Michigan Summers:

Tales & Recipes

Edited by Carole Eberly

eberly press
1004 Michigan Ave.
E. Lansing, MI 48823

Printed in Michigan

ISBN 0-932296-14-9

To Jessica

About the Cover

These bathing beauties, along with a few gentlemen friends and a dog, posed for this shot in 1890 along Lake Michigan near South Haven. (Photos in this book are courtesy of the State Archives of Michigan.)

A summer picnic, circa 1898, in the Lansing area called for elaborate hats.

Table of Contents

*What better way to spend a summer afternoon in the
1950s than swimming near Stephenson?*

Comic Books
and
Wax Gum

By Carole Eberly

One of the reasons I love Michigan so much is because summer is summer, winter is winter, spring is spring and autumn is autumn. No doubt about it. No wimpy 70-degree winters. No balmy, 65-degree summers--at least where most of us live. And everything in between prepares you for what is to follow. Only the hardiest survive.

My fondest memories of summer are in the pre-air conditioned mall days of the 1940s and 1950s. Summer consisted of walking up-town to drink cherry cokes for a nickel at the drug store, exploring the riverbank behind my house for Indian arrow heads and riding my bike to the Seashore Pool in Dearborn. No planned activities--except an occasional picnic at Belle Isle with a Leonard Smith concert afterward and our annual trips to Bob-Lo and the Detroit Zoo. Certainly no--God forbid--educational programs. No nothing. Just waking up each day to...well, nothing. If things reached the boredom level, mom always had one suggestion--clean your room. It was her own Head Start program. If you got a head start, you could be out of the house before she brought the subject up again.

And there was always the mandatory odyssey "up north." No one has ever actually located "up north," but every Michigander knows where it is. It's "up north."

Preparations for our one-week vacation began a month prior to the trip. Mom would clean the house from the curtains to the kitchen floor, making it socially acceptable to any burglar who wanted to break into

7

a modest brick bungalow. Clothes were packed in suit-cases. Bedding and towels found comfortable homes in boxes. Food, just in case there was none "up north," rattled around in brown paper A&P bags. Then, of course, there were the mandatory Monopoly and Rook games, fishing rods and AAA maps.

It's a good thing my dad was an engineer be-cause it took all his skills to cram this junk into our maroon Studebaker. Besides that, he had to figure out how to get my brother and I to sit next to each other in the back seat. This was no easy task since Bill and I, in true sibling tradition, were known to begin poking and elbowing matches before my father even shifted into second gear.

Ah, but once the long trip was over.... The musty smell of the cabin near Elk Rapids could never be matched by all the perfumeries in Paris. The ice box hung together on the front porch, the sagging beds sagged a little more than the year before, four mis-matched chairs completed the dining set. Heaven.

"Race ya to the beach," were the first words out of my brother's mouth. Carefully packed clothes went flying around the room in search of bathing suits.

Days were spent at the beach, reading books on the front porch or just hanging around town. The drug store was a favorite haunt because it contained comic books and three-inch-high wax bottles filled with red, green and purple syrup. While reading "Archie" and "Superman" comic books at the rack, Bill and I bit off the tops of the bottles and drank the liquid, finest vin-tage. Then we popped the bottles into our mouths and chewed them like gum. Actually, they tasted more like the paraffin mom put on jelly jars, but what the heck. We were "up north" and things were naturally better.

One day we picked some red cherries along the road to lug home. Mom made the best cherry pie I tasted--before or since--with an oven that had seen more of a workout than an Interstate Wendy's grill.

Bill and dad went fishing every so often. They even caught a fish once. I found it flopping around the kitchen floor as it escaped the pail searching for a way back to the stream. Dad heard my screams and promptly collared the poor fellow, filleting him on the spot. I couldn't eat much that night.

Evenings found us around the kitchen table playing Monopoly, each trying to land on Boardwalk first. You just KNEW whoever bought Boardwalk would win the game. You could be up to your ears in mortgages, picking up a "Go Directly to Jail, Do Not Pass Go" card, and out of money. But not to worry. Sooner or later Boardwalk would come through.

We even got to drink Rock 'n Rye on those evenings. At home it was always Vernor's down at the Detroit plant, watching the bottling taking place. But "up north" was Rock 'n Rye territory. Bags of pretzels and New Era potato chips topped off this gluttonous travel into gourmet-land.

Ah, summer. No wonder teachers went crazy around May.

The Queen's Float at Traverse City's annual National Cherry Festival Parade in 1935.

APPETIZERS & BEVERAGES

MICHIGAN PATE

1/2 pound chicken livers
1/4 cup butter
4 ounces halved fresh mushrooms
2 chopped green onions
1/4 cup sherry
1 teaspoon salt
Dash pepper

Saute chicken livers in butter until tender. Put into blender with remaining ingredients. Process until smooth. Spoon into a small crock and refrigerate overnight. (Makes about 1 1/2 cups.)

SMOKED WHITEFISH PATE

3/4 pound smoked whitefish, skinned and boned
1 8-ounce package cream cheese
3 tablespoons lemon juice
2 tablespoons cream
1 clove minced garlic
1/4 teaspoon salt

Finely chop fish so it makes about 1 1/2 cups. Thoroughly combine with remaining ingredients. Chill. Serve with crackers. (Makes about 2 cups.)

EGG AND BACON DIP

1 8-ounce package cream cheese
4 finely chopped hard boiled eggs
4 strips crisp fried bacon, crumbled
1 small chopped dill pickle
1/2 medium green pepper, seeded and chopped
1/2 cup chopped green onions
1 tablespoon milk
1/2 teaspoon celery salt
Pepper to taste

Mix all ingredients together. Chill at least two hours. Serve with crackers. (Makes about 3 cups.)

PINCONNING CHEESE DIP

1/4 cup water
1 cup creamed cottage cheese
2 3-ounce packages cream cheese
2 tablespoons chili sauce
1/4 teaspoon celery salt
1/4 small onion
1 tablespoon Worcestershire sauce
1 cup diced Pinconning cheese

Put water and cottage cheese into blender and process until smooth. Add remaining ingredients, except cheese and process until smooth. Gradually add the cheese, blending until smooth. (Makes about 2 cups.)

SPICY VEGETABLE DIP

4 medium tomatoes, peeled and finely chopped
1/4 cup finely chopped onion
1/4 cup finely chopped green pepper
3 tablespoons finely chopped green chilies
1/4 cup olive oil
2 tablespoons red wine vinegar
1 teaspoon mustard seed
1/4 teaspoon garlic salt
Dash pepper

Mix all ingredients together and chill thoroughly before serving. Serve with raw vegetables or corn chips. (Makes about 1 1/2 cups.)

EGGPLANT APPETIZER

1/4 cup olive oil
1 cup chopped onion
3 cloves minced garlic
1 medium eggplant, peeled and chopped
2 green peppers, seeded and chopped
1 cup chopped mushrooms
1 medium tomato, peeled and diced
2 tablespoons red wine vinegar
1/4 cup light brown sugar
1/2 teaspoon crushed basil
Salt and pepper to taste

Saute onion and garlic in olive oil until tender. Add eggplant, green pepper and tomato. Cover and cook, stirring occasionally, for about 15 minutes. Add vinegar, brown sugar and basil. Simmer uncovered for another 15 minutes, or until all ingredients are tender. Season with salt and pepper. Add more vinegar if you like it with more zip. Serve at room temperature with Italian bread. (Makes 4 to 8 servings.)

DEVILED EGGS

6 hard boiled eggs
3 finely chopped green onions
3 tablespoons mayonnaise
1 tablespoon Dijon mustard
Salt and pepper to taste
Paprika

Cut eggs in half lengthwise. Scoop out the yolks and mash. Mix with all ingredients, except paprika. Put mixture back into egg whites. Sprinkle with paprika. Chill until ready to serve.

ZUCCHINI-CHEESE SQUARES

3 cups shredded zucchini
1 cup Bisquick
4 beaten eggs
1/2 cup olive oil
1/2 cup shredded Parmesan cheese
1/2 cup chopped onion
2 cloves minced garlic
2 tablespoons chopped parsley
1 teaspoon Italian seasoning
1/2 teaspoon oregano
Salt and pepper to taste

Mix all ingredients together. Pour into a greased 13x9-inch pan. Bake at 350 degrees for 35 minutes or until light brown. Cool slightly. Cut into 24 squares.

SPINACH AND CHEESE SQUARES

(Even spinach-haters will love these. The squares freeze well in plastic bags.)

1/2 cup butter
3 eggs
1 cup flour
1 cup milk
1 teaspoon baking powder
1 teaspoon salt
1 pound shredded Monterey Jack cheese
4 cups chopped spinach

Melt butter in a 9x13-inch pan. Beat eggs in a large bowl. Mix in flour, milk, baking powder and salt. Stir in remaining ingredients. Pour into the pan and bake at 350 degrees for 40 minutes. Cool 30 minutes before cutting into 45 squares. Serve hot or cold.

STRAWBERRY FRUIT DRINK

(You may also substitute 1 cup of water for the milk, if you wish.

3/4 cup strawberries
1 cup milk
2 tablespoons sugar
1 cup crushed ice

Put all ingredients into blender and process until smooth. Makes 2 cups.)

RASPBERRY BREAKFAST

1 cup cold milk
1 egg
1/2 cup raspberries
1/4 teaspoon vanilla

Put all ingredients into blender and process until smooth. (Makes 1 serving.)

BLACK CHERRY ICE CREAM SODA

3 tablespoons milk
1/3 cup black cherries
2 scoops vanilla or black cherry ice cream, divided
Ginger ale

Put milk, cherries and 1 scoop of ice cream into blender and process until smooth. Pour into a tall glass. Add another scoop of ice cream. Slowly fill glass with ginger ale. (Makes 1 serving.)

RED CHERRY SHAKE

1 cup cold milk
2 scoops vanilla ice cream
3 tablespoons sugar
1/2 cup red cherries

Put all ingredients into blender and process until smooth. (Makes 2 cups.)

TOMATO JUICE COCKTAIL

1 quart tomato juice
4 tablespoons lemon juice
4 tablespoons Worcestershire sauce
1 tablespoon Tabasco sauce
1/2 teaspoon celery salt
Pepper to taste

Combine all ingredients. Chill before serving. (Makes about 1 quart.)

PEACH DAIQUIRI

1 medium unpeeled peach, cut into chunks
3 ounces light rum
4 teaspoons sugar
Juice of one lime
1/2 cup crushed ice

Put all ingredients into blender and process until mixed and thick. Garnish with a peach slice. (Makes four drinks.)

PLUM CORDIAL

1 quart vodka
3 pounds plums, pitted and quartered
2 1/2 cups sugar
2 vanilla beans, split lengthwise

Mix all ingredients together and pour into a gallon jar. Cover. Stir daily for one week. Stir once a week thereafter. Strain and bottle after 3 months. (Makes 1 1/4 quarts.)

MICHIGAN KIR

(You can also use blackberry brandy or cherry bounce in place of the plum cordial.)

Plum cordial
Champagne or light, fruity white wine

Pour about two tablespoons of cordial into wine glass. Fill with chilled champagne or wine.

A typical 1960s beach scene at any state park. This one happens to be the Tawas State Park. Is that Sandra Dee in the foreground? What is that boy with the binoculars looking at? Who is that man in the black shoes?

"Up North"
Before I-75

By Peter Marabell

In the REAL old days--before the interstate high-way system connected every city, town and village in the state that had sufficient clout with the Highway Department--the drive from Detroit to Mackinaw City boiled down to two choices: long and very long.

Choosing the "long" way entailed finding US-16 as it aimed its way northwest out of downtown Detroit, shooting through Brighton, Howell, and Williamston, before it turned right at Lansing and headed north on US-27.

US-16 used to wind its way through the northern tier of states, the Bad Lands of the Dakotas, Montana, and Utah before it deadened at the Pacific Ocean. It's gone now, but signs that proclaim "Old Grand River" or "Old 16" suggest that US-16 lives on in some lesser incarnation. Most of US-16 has been replaced, at least in Michigan, by Interstate-96.

For the ride north from Lansing, US-27 is alive...except in places where other parallel roads are still called, for obscure reasons, "Old 27," or "Old 27 North." Inevitably, as you might guess, US-27 comes to a rather ingloriously end as a strip for Grayling's fast food restaurants and discount shoe stores. The final 85 miles to Mackinaw City is the domain of I-75, that noble testament to human technological genius that enables us to leave the Keys wearing our bathing suits and motor to the land of ice hockey without interruption should our bladders be large enough. Of course, there are any number of "Old 27s" and "Old 27 Norths" along the way should nostalgia for the simple appeal of the good ole days take over.

If all this sounds a bit confusing, sit back and pour another cup of coffee and consider the myriad of spellings and pronunciations for Mackinaw...er...Mackinac. It's really quite amazing where debate will settle down and make trouble. The always heated, and I might add, silly controversy comes down to the pronunciation of that nasty little "c." On any number of occasions, I've seen otherwise classy, intelligent women and men--that leaves out Democrats and Republicans--stand nose-to-nose shouting "ack" or "awe" at the end of each "Mackin..."

These "discussions" go on far too long, until the whitefish dinner gets so cold that it's no longer appetizing. Curiously, it's usually tourists who engage in this kind of revelry. Locals are happy to agree with which ever pronunciation results in a larger fudge buy. One steamy night a few years back, I overheard a conversation, in the bar at the old Dixie Tavern, in which four locals--fudge dealers all--described in exquisite detail the relationship between the volume of the "ack-awe" debate and the size of the subsequent drug...er... fudge buy.

A brief sidebar in history. The Dixie Tavern in Mackinaw City is gone now, replaced by the only McDonald's allowed to close six months of the year. Really warms the heart, doesn't it?

Back on US-27, the earliest road signs proclaiming what was to come appeared north of Higgins Lake as one ferry company or another touted that it had the biggest, or smallest, or quietest, or cheapest, or longest, or safest, or smoothest boats to Mackinac Island. While the companies could never agree on whose boats could do what, they had no trouble at all agreeing on the price of a round-trip ticket. Legend has it that before Teddy Roosevelt busted the oil and steel trusts, he studied the Mackinaw Island ferry companies so he could fully comprehend the intricacies of price-fixing.

The motor trip of this reasonably direct route took six hours, more or less. It was usually more, unless my father had recently taken the wheel of a powerful new Pontiac or Buick. Then "more" truly became "less."

If we weren't in a hurry--and before the super-slabs, no one was EVER successfully in a hurry--US-23 came north out of Toledo almost knicking the western suburbs of Detroit as it climbed its way to Saginaw Bay. Then it meandered--good God, did it ever meander--its way along the Lake Huron shore to Mackinaw City. Seeing the lake did indeed make the trip prettier, but aesthetics can mask torture for only so long. An endless succession of slowdowns, otherwise called villages, souvenir or fresh fruit stands, and scenic turnouts, were more than enough to have made me car-sick, but my father flung his new Pontiac from village to village with such reckless abandon that I was too busy hanging on to be car-sick.

The first indication that we were "up north" came as we passed through Pinconning, which if you believe the signs has more cheese available for consumption than the Dutch. Of course, you could never prove it by me because the word "Pinconning" has never appeared in crossword puzzles, which are essential for learning about cheese.

And so we rode on, through Standish, Tawas (and heaven help us, there were TWO of those) to the thriving metropolis of Alpena. On Michigan's Huron shore, any gathering of people is a metropolis, and it would be dubbed "thriving" if it had three souvenir stands, two gas stations, an authentic Indian teepee, and at least one renegade fireworks stand touting "genuine" Ohio firecrackers.

By the time we passed Rogers City, our spirits were buoyed in the knowledge that we had only 90 minutes left...unless the drawbridge was up in Cheboygan. And it was. Every time.

This version of the northern trek, the scenic route I think it was called, took longer than six hours... about three days longer.

And another thing. Whenever we took the scenic route, we always arrived after dark...even though we left Detroit at 5:30 a.m. and made only two stops (one for the bathroom, one for cheese). This curious fact has haunted me for so many years that one day I entered all the data into my trusty home computer. No matter how I calculated, manipulated, or cajoled it, the answers spit out always told me the same thing: driving time from Detroit to Mackinaw City takes less than the

15 hours of available daylight. Nonetheless, we always arrived after dark. I think Ingmar Bergman made a movie about it sometime back. It was called "To The Straits Darkly." It tells the story of voluptuous but lonely Cheboygan woman who meets a blond-haired, blue-eyed Swedish freighter captain at Snoopy's Bar late one fall night...but I digress too much.

The drive north today simply doesn't compare with the good old days. There's little adventure in today's sophisticated, cushy environment. For Pete's sake, what does it take? We jump in the highway cruiser, set the electrically heated seats, adjust the temperature control, hit the road and set the auto-pilot, flip on the radar detector, pop a New-Age CD into the stereo and arrive with nary a hair or nerve out of place.

Unless, of course, we tried to take our cruiser through that rolling log-jam called Zilwaukee. I remain convinced that the traffic bottleneck that engulfs Zilwaukee was designed intentionally by a vengeful little man who deeply resented how often he was forced to listen to the village fathers say, "Build your freeway over here! Our economy needs help."

And finally, by which ever route, we arrived in Mackinaw City. At that moment, waiting for the ferry to the Island, nothing else mattered because the promise of summer is always the same: sun and sailing, cars and friends, romance and adventure. In days gone by, it was the land of the French, then the British, always native Americans, and now...seemingly forever...tourists, called "fudgies" by the locals. There are forts and parks, souvenirs and food, a magical island and a dazzling bridge. There are skeletons of wrecked ships just 20 feet below the surface of the water. And there is fudge, oh my, is there fudge! Where fudge and tourists meet, where Lakes Huron and Michigan splash against one another, the spirit is forever young. The adventures of children remain the adventures of the light-hearted...at the Straits of Mackinaw.

Hey, let's all have fun in the Dune Scooter! These people did in the 1940s at Silver Lake.

SOUPS & SALADS

CREAM OF SPINACH SOUP

3 tablespoons butter
1/4 cup chopped onions
4 tablespoons flour
1 1/2 pounds cooked and chopped spinach
2 1/2 cups chicken broth
1 1/2 cups milk
Salt and pepper to taste
1 cup cream

Saute onions in butter until tender. Blend in flour until smooth. Slowly add stock and milk. Bring to a boil, stirring constantly. Reduce heat. Add spinach, salt and pepper. Stir in cream being careful not to boil. (Makes 4-6 servings.)

ICED TOMATO SOUP

2 cups tomato juice
1 cup cream
3 tablespoon sherry
Salt and pepper to taste
2 teaspoons brown sugar
Minced parsley

Combine all ingredients, except parsley, together. Chill thoroughly. Pour into serving bowls and sprinkle with parsley. (Makes 4 servings.)

CHILLED CUCUMBER-BUTTERMILK SOUP

7 cups buttermilk
3 tablespoons chopped chives
1 peeled cucumber, seeded and diced
1 teaspoon dill
3 tablespoons chopped parsley
Salt and pepper to taste

Stir buttermilk and chives together and let stand for 30 minutes. Mix cucumber, dill and parsley together and let stand for 30 minutes. Combine all ingredients with salt and pepper. Chill thoroughly. (Makes 6-8 servings.)

ICED CARROT SOUP

4 cups chicken broth
6 carrots, cut in chunks
1 large sliced onion
3/4 teaspoon salt
Large dash dried thyme
1/2 cup cream
Salt and pepper to taste
Chopped parsley

Bring stock, carrot, onion, salt and thyme to a boil. Reduce heat and simmer for 30 minutes. Place carrots, onion and some of the broth into a blender and process until smooth. Remove broth from heat. Return carrot mixture to broth and stir in cream. Stir in salt and pepper. Chill thoroughly. Sprinkle with parsley before serving.

VICHYSSOISE ICE CREAM

(If you have an ice cream maker on hand, here is an unusual recipe to try.)

2 chopped green onions
1 tablespoon butter
1 cup chicken stock
1 medium chopped potato
2 teaspoons unflavored, softened gelatin
1 1/2 cups whipping cream
2 tablespoons chopped chives
Salt and pepper to taste

Saute onions in butter until tender. Add to potato, gelatin and chicken broth, simmering 30 minutes. Process in blender until smooth. Stir in cream, chives, salt and pepper. Chill one hour. Churn away. Eat.

CREAM OF CELERY SOUP

1 1/2 cups diced celery
2 tablespoons chopped celery leaves
2 cups water
2 tablespoons butter
2 tablespoons flour
2 cups milk
Salt and pepper to taste

Cook the celery and leaves in water until celery is tender, about 20 minutes. Melt butter in a saucepan and stir in the flour. Gradually add the milk, stirring constantly until mixture is smooth. Stir in the celery, cooking liquid, salt and pepper. Simmer for 10 minutes, stirring frequently. (Makes 4 servings.)

CHILLED BLUEBERRY SOUP

3 cups water
1 quart blueberries
3/4 cup sugar
1/2 teaspoon cinnamon
2 tablespoons cornstarch
2 tablespoons cold water
Sour cream

Boil water in a saucepan. Stir in blueberries, sugar and cinnamon, cooking until sugar dissolves. Mix cornstarch with cold water in a cup. Stir into berry mixture and bring to a boil. Chill thoroughly. Serve with a spoonful of sour cream on top of each serving. (Makes 6-8 servings.)

CHILLED CHUNKY TOMATO SOUP

(Definitely different.)

1 tablespoon unflavored gelatin
1/2 cup cold water
2 cups tomato juice
1 tablespoon Worcestershire sauce
Chopped parsley

Mix gelatin and water in a saucepan and let stand for 5 minutes. Add 1 cup tomato juice, stirring over heat until gelatin dissolves. Add remaining tomato juice and Worcestershire sauce, mixing well. Pour into an 8x8-inch pan. Chill until firm. Cut into small cubes and serve in glass bowls. Sprinkle with parsley. (Makes 2-4 servings.)

TOMATO-BUTTERMILK SOUP

2 cups peeled and chopped tomatoes
1 cup buttermilk
1 cloves minced garlic
1 tablespoon chopped onion
1/4 teaspoon dried basil
Salt and pepper to taste

Process all ingredients in blender until almost smooth. Chill. (Makes 4 servings.)

GAZPACHO

(One of my favorites, I keep a pitcher full of this in my fridge all summer. I like it because, besides the basic vegetables mentioned here, I can use most any veggies around. Also, I can change the taste by experimenting with various seasonings. Not only that, but it keeps a long time and is easy to make.)

1 medium cubed onion
1 cubed and seeded green pepper
1 cubed cucumber
2 cloves garlic
1 tablespoon olive oil
1/4 cup white wine vinegar
2 tablespoons Worcestershire sauce
Dash (or two) of Tabasco sauce
1 teaspoon salt
1/8 teaspoon fresh ground pepper
6 peeled tomatoes
2 cups tomato juice, divided

Chop everything but tomatoes in a food processor or blender with a small amount of the tomato juice for 10 to 20 seconds. Pour half the mixture into a bowl. Chop the tomatoes with the remaining vegetables in the food processor. Pour into the bowl with the other vegetables. Add remaining tomato juice and stir well. Chill thoroughly. Garnish with croutons or parsley or whatever else you have on hand. (Makes 6-8 servings.)

SAUERKRAUT SALAD

1 1-pound, 11-ounce can sauerkraut
3/4 cup sugar
1 cup diced green pepper
1 cup diced celery
1/4 cup diced onion
3 tablespoons vinegar
1/4 teaspoon salt
1/8 teaspoon pepper
2 tablespoons diced pimentos

Drain sauerkraut well. Mix all ingredients together in a large bowl. Cover and chill overnight. (Makes 8-10 servings.

VEGETABLE-COTTAGE CHEESE SALAD

1 cup water
1/2 cup olive oil
1/2 cup lemon juice
1 teaspoon onion salt
1 teaspoon oregano
1/2 teaspoon dried basil
1 clove minced garlic
Dash of pepper
2 cups carrot sticks
2 cups zucchini sticks
2 cups cauliflower
Cottage cheese

Heat to a boil the water, olive oil, lemon juice, onion salt, oregano, basil, garlic and pepper. Stir in vegetables and boil about 4 minutes. Chill vegetables in marinade at least three hours. Drain and serve vegetables over individual servings of cottage cheese. (Makes 4 servings.)

SPINACH-COTTAGE CHEESE SALAD

(A good make-ahead salad. Just be sure the spinach is fresh--frozen won't work.)

1 6-ounce package of lemon gelatin
1 1/2 teaspoon vinegar
2 cups boiling water
1/2 cup mayonnaise
1/2 pound chopped spinach
1/2 cup celery
3 tablespoons chopped onion
1/2 pound cottage cheese

Stir together gelatin, vinegar, water and mayonnaise. Let stand until partially set. Mix in remaining ingredients. Chill in an 8x8-inch pan until firm. Cut into 9 cubes. (Makes 9 servings.)

GERMAN SPINACH SALAD

1 pound fresh spinach leaves, stems removed
6 slices diced bacon
1/4 cup vinegar
1/4 cup sugar
1/2 teaspoon mustard
2 hard boiled eggs, peeled and sliced

Wash and drain spinach leaves. Tear into bite-sized pieces in salad bowl. Fry bacon until crisp. Pour all but 1/4 cup of the grease out of the pan. Stir in the vinegar, sugar and mustard, heating to a boil. Pour over spinach leaves. Garnish with egg slices. Serve immediately. (Makes 4 to 6 servings.)

COLESLAW

1 large head shredded cabbage
2 large shredded carrots
1 large shredded green pepper
1/2 medium shredded onion
1 cup mayonnaise (more or less)
3 tablespoons vinegar
1 teaspoon sugar
Salt and pepper to taste

Mix vegetables together in a salad bowl. Mix remaining ingredients together. Add dressing to vegetables and combine well. You may need to adjust the mayonnaise according to the amount of vegetables. (Makes 8 to 10 servings.)

BRUSSELS SPROUTS SALAD

1 pound Brussels sprouts, halved
1 small chopped onion
1/2 cup chopped cooked beets
1 cup salad oil
1/4 cup red wine vinegar
1 teaspoon Dijon mustard
1 teaspoon Worcestershire sauce
1 teaspoon sugar
1 teaspoon salt
2 teaspoons chopped fresh basil
1/4 teaspoon ground pepper

Boil sprouts until just tender, about 7 minutes. Drain and mix in a bowl with onion and beets. Mix remaining ingredients together. Pour over vegetables and chill thoroughly, stirring occasionally. (Makes 4 servings.)

BACK-YARD GARDEN SALAD BOWL

2 cups sliced carrots
2 cups cauliflowerettes
2 cups broccoli
2 cups green beans, cut into 1-inch pieces
2 cups sliced zucchini
1 green seeded pepper, cut into strips
1 red seeded red pepper, cut into strips
6 sliced green onions

Bring a large pot of water to a boil. Add the carrots and cook 1 minute. Add the cauliflowerettes and broccoli, cooking 1 more minute. Add the green beans, cooking 1 more minute. Add the zucchini and cook 1 minute more. Drain well. Mix vegetables in a large bowl with green pepper and onions. Pour your favorite Italian or oil and vinegar-type dressing over and mix well. Chill thoroughly, stirring occasionally. (Makes a lot of servings.)

GOOD OLD POTATO SALAD

(Is a summer complete without potato salad? Not according to my mom.)

3 cups sliced cooked potatoes
1/2 cup chopped onion
3/4 cup mayonnaise
2 sliced hard boiled eggs
1 teaspoon parsley
Salt and pepper to taste
Paprika

Mix potatoes with onion and mayonnaise. Gently fold in eggs and parsley. Season with salt and pepper. Sprinkle paprika on top. Chill thoroughly. (Makes 4 servings.)

Martha's Chewing Taffy--or is it, Martha is chewing taffy--at the 1945 Ingham County Fair in Mason.

Zucchini:
Have Some--
PLEASE

By Robert Clock

"Rape!" I cried hoarsely, stumbling in the back door, my arms laden with provender from the garden. "It's a case of rape, pure and simple!"

"Who was raped?" Judy mumbled cheerily, entering the kitchen from the sewing room with her mouth full of straight pins.

"You remember that pretty little cucumber vine back by the raspberry patch?" I asked, dumping my booty on the kitchen counter, "The one with the little yellow flowers all over it?"

"How could I forget!" Judy answered. "I tripped over it every time I picked berries this summer. I told you not to plant cucumbers so close to the raspberries."

"What I was trying to do was to keep the cucumbers as far as possible from the zucchini, but it didn't work. Look what happened," I said, waving a misshapen green object the size of a bowling pin under her nose. "What do you call that?"

Judy examined the strange object. "It looks like a pregnant cucumber."

"Pretty close," I said. "It came off the cucumber vine, but it's a zucumber or a cucchini--the illegitimate offspring of an illicit union between that big macho zucchini plant in the middle of the garden and that pretty little cucumber vine. Have you ever seen such a strange looking vegetable?"

"I wonder what it tastes like," Judy mused.

In a minute I had it peeled and sliced. The dry pulp inside was almost tasteless.

37

"That settles it," I said flatly. "Next summer--no zucchini. I've said it before, but this time I mean it. Can you imagine that rotten zucchini out there cross-breeding behind our backs? When you have to hire a full-time chaperone to prevent hanky-panky in the garden patch, things have gone too far."

Twenty-five years ago zucchini posed no problems for the average, native-born American gardener because he had never heard of it. Then in the early 1950s, Americans discovered Italian food. Pizza palaces reared their neon signs from Maine to California, spaghetti factories put on extra hands, "antipasto" ceased to be someone's relative and turned into a splendid salad. Lasagna, scaloppini, and cacciatore became household words.

It was fashionable to have "garlic breath."

I suppose it was inevitable that the national fetish for things Italian should lead eventually to the zucchini.

The first time I laid eyes on one of those gargantuan members of the squash family was in 1953 or 1954. My father belonged to a car pool with a gentlemen of Italian extraction who did a little gardening in his spare time. One day my father returned from work with a 25-pound zucchini on his shoulder. My mother and I gathered around to watch as he laid it gently on the kitchen table. It looked like it was made of plastic.

"What is it?" my mother asked, keeping her distance.

"I forget," dad answered. "It has a funny Italian name. Luigi grew it in his backyard. He says we can have more if we want them."

"How do you fix it?"

"He didn't say."

We used it as a hassock until it started to smell bad.

It was only a matter of time before American gardeners became afflicted with zucchini madness--driven to experiment more out of curiosity than by a raging passion for the bland vegetable itself. The first growers borrowed seeds from their Italian neighbors. The commercial seed packers joined the act and before you could say Garibaldi, the entire American landscape was overrun with zucchini vines.

I think we were simply overwhelmed by a garden plant that germinates while your back is turned, grows three or four inches while you are looking for the watering can, and produces dozens of immense, elongated vegetables that would be obscene in any other context.

Unfortunately, zucchini appears to have no natural enemies on this side of the Atlantic. I have never heard of a plant dying from anything except old age, frostbite or physical violence.

Zucchini would be easier to accept as a dietary staple if the species weren't so fertile. One plant, for example, will produce enough zucchini to satisfy the needs of an entire neighborhood. Plant two seeds and you become a truck gardener.

Yet some novice gardeners make the mistake of planting an entire package of seeds in one season. A friend who put in his first garden last summer committed this awful error. His poor wife, a very frugal woman who hated to see such a bountiful harvest go to waste, attempted to serve a different zucchini dish every evening; sauteed zucchini the first night, zucchini pancakes the next. Then zucchini spaghetti casserole, batter fried zucchini, steamed zucchini, zucchini strips with dip.

On the seventh day, without a smidgen of remorse, my friend went out to the garden with a baseball bat and clubbed his zucchini plants to death.

Other growers are not tough enough to commit murder. Instead they try to give their harvest away. It is pitiful to see them trudging through the streets, a gigantic green squash under each arm, asking total strangers if they like zucchini.

With three-quarters of the world's population going to bed hungry every night, you'd think there would be some willing takers, wouldn't you? But there aren't.

I know one zucchini grower who hides his surplus vegetables under the vines in neighboring gardens at night in hopes that someone will be able to use them.

There's another fellow in town who goes about after dark with a grocery bag of zucchini, leaving them on doorsteps like unwanted foundlings.

Last summer a neighbor made the mistake of going on vacation just as his zucchini were beginning to ripen. When he returned his entire yard was overrun with squash. He couldn't eat them or give them away, so he sold the house at a fraction of its market value.

The situation is so bad that a federal program plainly is needed to stamp out zucchini before another growing season rolls around. A federally funded sex education course for cucumbers also seems to be in order.

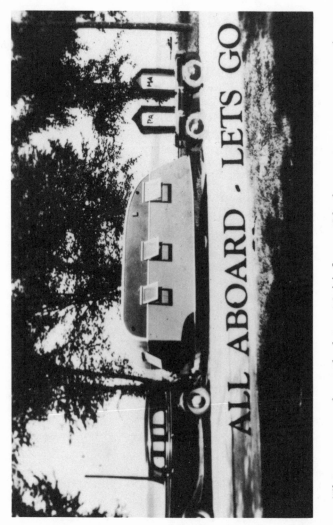

This postcard mailed in 1944 from Chelsea was sure to make someone back home envious.

SAUCES & JAMS

CUCUMBER-YOGURT SALAD DRESSING

1 1/2 cups plain yogurt
1 1/2 cups olive oil
3 tablespoons lemon juice
1/2 cup cucumber, peeled, seeded and grated
3 tablespoons grated onion
1 tablespoon chopped mint
1 tablespoon chopped parsley
Salt and pepper to taste

Mix yogurt, olive oil and lemon juice until smooth. Stir in remaining ingredients. Chill at least six hours. (Makes about 2 1/2 cups.)

PESTO SAUCE

1/4 lb. basil leaves
2 cloves of garlic
1/4 cup olive oil, divided
4 tablespoons grated Parmesan cheese
Melted butter

Place basil, garlic, 2 tablespoons olive oil and cheese in a blender. Blend until well chopped, but not mushy. Stir in remaining oil. If on the dry side, add a little melted butter. Serve over hot linguini. (Makes 4 servings.)

CHUNKY TOMATO SAUCE

3 tablespoons olive oil
1 large chopped onion
5 minced garlic cloves
6 pounds peeled and chopped tomatoes
2 teaspoons salt
1/2 cup chopped fresh basil leaves
1/2 teaspoon dried oregano
1/4 teaspoon fresh ground pepper
1/4 cup chopped fresh parsley

Saute onions and garlic in oil until onions are tender. Mix in tomatoes, salt, basil and oregano. Bring to a slight boil and cook uncovered, stirring frequently, until sauce is thickened, about 20-30 minutes. Add pepper and parsley. Sauce can be refrigerated for several days or frozen. (Makes about 3 pints.)

BARBECUE SAUCE

3 tablespoons oil
1 medium chopped onion
4 minced garlic cloves
3 tablespoons chopped fresh basil leaves
Large pinch of dried thyme
2 pounds peeled tomatoes, seeded and chopped
4 tablespoons Worcestershire sauce
3 tablespoons brown sugar
1/3 cup red wine vinegar
3 teaspoons Dijon mustard
1/2 teaspoon salt
1/2 teaspoon Tabasco sauce

Saute onion, garlic, basil and thyme in oil until onions are tender. Add remaining ingredients and bring to a boil. Lower heat and simmer uncovered, stirring frequently, until thickened, about 20-30 minutes. Refrigerated, this sauce will keep for several weeks. Use as a baste for chicken or ribs. (Makes 2-3 cups.)

PICKLED BEETS

4 1/2 cups sliced cooked beets
1 sliced medium onion
1/2 cup water
1/2 cup vinegar
4 tablespoons sugar
1/2 teaspoon salt

Place beets and onion in a bowl and mix. Combine remaining ingredients in saucepan and bring to a boil. Pour vinegar mixture over beets. Cover and refrigerate overnight. Serve cold. (Makes 6 servings.)

PICKLED CANTALOUPE

6 cups peeled cantaloupe
1 1/2 teaspoons alum
2 quarts water
2 cups sugar
2 cups vinegar
2 sticks cinnamon
2 teaspoons whole cloves

Cut cantaloupe into pieces 1 1/2 inches long by 1/2-inch thick. Set aside. Dissolve alum in water and bring to a boil. Add cantaloupe and boil for 15 minutes. Drain. Combine remaining ingredients with the cantaloupe and simmer slowly until clear, about 20 minutes. Remove cinnamon and cloves. Ladle into sterilized canning jars. (Makes about 5 half pints.)

BELL PEPPER RELISH

3/4 pound peeled onions
3 large green or red bell peppers, seeded
1 cup white vinegar
3/4 cup sugar
1 1/2 teaspoons salt
3/4 teaspoon mustard seeds

Cut onions and peppers into 1-inch chunks and place in a saucepan with other ingredients. Bring to a boil, stirring constantly. Reduce heat and boil uncovered, until reduced by a third, stirring often. (Makes 8 servings.)

WATERMELON PICKLES

2 quarts peeled watermelon rind
1/2 cup salt dissolved in 2 quarts of water
1/2 teaspoon powdered alum
1 quart white wine vinegar
6 pounds white sugar
1 ounce whole cinnamon
1 tablespoon whole cloves

Cut watermelon into squares. Cover in a kettle with salt water and let stand overnight. Drain and rinse. Cover with cold water mixed with the alum. Cook until tender, 8-10 minutes. Drain again. Cook vinegar, sugar, cinnamon and cloves 5 minutes, stirring constantly. Add drained rind. Boil gently until rind is transparent, about 30-40 minutes. Remove cinnamon and cloves. Ladle into sterilized jars. Let stand about 4 weeks before using. (Makes about 5 half pints.)

RED PEPPER JAM

2 cups grated flesh and liquid of
red bell peppers, about 6
3 cups sugar
1 cup apple cider vinegar
1/4 cup lemon juice
6 ounces liquid pectin

Combine red pepper flesh and liquid, sugar, vinegar and lemon juice in a saucepan. Boil, stirring to dissolve sugar. Bring to a full rolling boil. Stir in pectin and boil hard for 1 minute. Remove from heat and ladle into sterilized canning jars. Process for 10 minutes. Excellent on crackers or bagels spread first with cream cheese. (Makes 5 half pints.)

EASY MINT SAUCE

1 ounce water
8 teaspoons dried mint
4 tablespoons sugar
5 tablespoons vinegar

Bring water, mint and sugar to a boil. Stir until sugar is dissolved. Remove from heat and add the vinegar.

BLUEBERRY-PEACH JAM

3 cups blueberries
2 cups peeled and pitted peaches
7 cups sugar
1 package fruit pectin
1/4 teaspoon cinnamon

Crush blueberries and put in a medium saucepan. Dice peaches and add to blueberries. Mix pectin and cinnamon in fruit and cook over high heat, stirring constantly, until mixture comes to a full boil. Add sugar all at once. Bring to a full, rolling boil and boil for 1 more minute, stirring constantly. Remove from heat. Skim and stir to remove foam. Ladle into hot jars and seal. (Makes 8 8-ounce jars.)

SPICY PEAR BUTTER

5 pounds cored, peeled and quartered pears
3 cups canned pear nectar
1 teaspoon cinnamon
Dash ground cloves and nutmeg
2 cups sugar
2 tablespoons lemon juice

Boil pears, nectar and spices for 3 minutes. Lower heat and simmer, stirring occasionally, about 25-35 minutes, or until pears are tender. Combine pear mixture and sugar in blender. Pour into a 9x13-inch baking dish and bake at 300 degrees for 2 hours, or until thick. Stir in lemon juice. Refrigerate up to 1 month. (Makes 6 half-pints.)

VERY BERRY SAUCE

1 pint raspberries
1 pint hulled strawberries
3 tablespoons sugar
3 tablespoons raspberry liqueur

Combine all ingredients in a blender. Strain out raspberry seeds. Chill. Serve over ice cream, cake or pudding. (Makes about 3 cups.)

BLACK AND BLUE SAUCE

3 cups blackberries
3 cups blueberries
1 cup water
2 1/2 cups sugar
1/2 cup corn syrup
1/4 teaspoon salt
Dash cinnamon
1 tablespoon cornstarch
2 tablespoons cold water
1 tablespoon lemon juice

Bring blackberries, blueberries and water to a boil. Simmer until berries are slightly softened, about 5-10 minutes. Add sugar, corn syrup, salt and cinnamon. Boil again. Mix cornstarch with cold water and stir into berries. Simmer until mixture is slightly thickened, about 5 minutes. Cool and stir in lemon juice. Serve hot or cold over pancakes, waffles, ice cream, cake or pudding. (Makes about 5 cups.)

FRESH PEACH SAUCE

3 medium unpeeled and sliced peaches
1 teaspoon ascorbic acid powder
1/2 cup sugar
Pinch of salt

Liquefy one peach in blender. Add ascorbic acid and process until smooth. Gradually add remaining ingredients, blending until smooth. Refrigerate or freeze. (Makes 2 cups.)

STEWED CHERRIES

1 pound ripe black cherries, pitted
1/2 cup sugar
1 cup water
2-inch stick cinnamon

Mix fruit and sugar in saucepan and let sit for 30 minutes. Stir in remaining ingredients, simmering gently for 10-16 minutes. Remove cherries with a slotted spoon. Let cooking liquid boil down to a medium-thick syrup. Stir cherries back into liquid. Serve hot over ice cream, cake or pudding, or plain with whipped cream. (Makes 6-8 servings.)

Nothing like a parade of elephants through town to get your attention. This was part of a 1908 circus in Cheboygan.

Circus-time
at the
Settlement

By Eugene Davenport

(The following is a piece written about pioneer Michigan in the 1860s. The settlement was located in the Grand River Valley, a heavily forested area of Southern Michigan.)

It was a red-letter day when Dan Rice came to the settlement with his little old one-ring circus. Not even the tricks of the sleight-of-hand performer who traveled about from schoolhouse to schoolhouse could compare with the wonders of the circus. When the magician pounded neighbor Smith's watch to flinders in a mortar then handed it back to him safe and sound, we knew there was hocus-pocus in it somewhere. But there was no deception in the elephant or the clown that Dan Rice brought to our neck of the woods one long-remembered day in early summer. They were real and they were wonderful.

It was before the railroads had reached our vicinity and the outfit traveled overland in wagons which transported the performers and the meager equipment, mostly tents and seats. Horses were the only animals except for the single elephant--he was not only a star performer in the ring but also on the roads. He often was called upon to push the wagons when they stalled in the mud.

One and only one bridge spanned the little river just outside our town. The elephant was started across to test the bridge's reliability. But after taking a few steps, he whistled and turned tail for the bank and safety. The decision of the elephant was instantly accepted as final. The alternative was to ford the stream near the place where we used to drive across in dry seasons to wet the fillies and set the tires of the wagon wheels lest they drop off as sometimes happened. Naturally we expected to see the teams double up as was customary with us when negotiating a particularly bad stretch of road.

Not at all. Before the eyes of all the astonished children gathered there, the wagons, one by one, went down into the drink, and the elephant sedately put his head to the rear and furnished all the necessary power, leaving the horse nothing to do but to provide steerage at the tongue. Wonderful that a single animal should have so much power in his body, brains in his head and a disposition to be accommodating!

There was no need of a street parade, for we had seen every step of the circus' progress into the settlement. The final preparations we watched with bated breath. The ring covered with sawdust! Three workmen driving together on the same stake! The monstrous tent going up!

Dan Rice was owner, manager, and clown. When the show opened there he was with the ringmaster, togged out with all the habiliments of the court fool, a marvelous sight in our eyes. Even so, the ringmaster was the cynosure of all eyes. Was it possible that any man could afford for every day such magnificent clothing as his Prince Albert coat and plug hat? What a figure he made with his long whip and his devil-may-care attitude toward the performers and all the world!

As a curtain-raiser the ringmaster and the clown entered into conversation about certain of the most prominent citizens of the town: Nate Barlow, Sol Goodyear, Lawyer Holbrook and Old Doc Upjohn. How in tunket had they ever become acquainted with these, our most prominent citizens? However, by this means they worked off their repertoire of standard jokes and the show began.

What a show! Such riding! Why, they actually stood up on the horses' backs when on the dead run! And one of them actually turned a somersault through a hoop covered with paper and came out all right on the other side on top of the horse! Half the boys of the settlement tried to ride bareback for weeks afterward, but nothing came of it except bumped noses and skinned elbows.

One of the mysteries never solved was the amount and kind of local information the clown read off the paper before the rider jumped through the hoop. How it ever got there was too much for us. Then there were the Australian Twins who did wonderful stunts on the horizontal bar, only we were saddened a bit by our parents' opinion, expressed freely and with the utmost assurance, that such people never lived long.

Now that first circus came just at the close of the Civil War, and Horace Greeley's editorials had been for years the political bible of the Black Republicans of the North. But Greeley's popularity had waned when he bailed Jeff Davis out of the Federal prison. The people of the timberland, indeed all the North, wanted Davis hung on the traditional sour apple tree. Anyhow Greeley suffered a fall from grace before even his most ardent admirers. From an oracle he became the butt of ridicule, fair game for a circus clown.

In those days every circus activity stopped when the clown wanted to say something to the ringmaster. So it was that in the midst of one of the most exciting moments he motioned to the ringmaster and every man and horse stopped in his tracks.

Clown: "Say, say, my Uncle John fell into the millpond last week. What d'y suppose he did?"

Ringmaster: "Why, waded ashore, of course."

Clown: "No, sir. Water too deep."

Ringmaster: "Then he must have swum to land."

Clown: "Not by a jugful. My uncle's too smart for that."

Ringmaster: "Well, what did he do?"

Clown: "Called for Horace Greeley, of course."

Ringmaster: "What did he want of him?"

Clown: "Why, to bail him out to be sure."

Then we all howled as we were expected to do, the clown turned a cartwheel, and the show went on.

One of the main attractions was an Arabian stallion. He was white as milk and it was some years before we learned that for show purposes any white horse was an Arabian. In plain truth this one was nothing but an albino. But he passed the test of the times and we took great stock in the fact that we had seen a real Arabian horse and a stallion at that. It was the first time I had ever heard the word "stallion."

This was before P. T. Barnum took to the road with various curiosities like the woolly horse and freaks like Edwin Smith, an old schoolmate of my father, who sported a real beard that swept the floor with some eighteen inches to spare; and General Tom Thumb, "twenty-two inches, boots, and all." I saw them and other and bigger shows, circus and menagerie combined with all the appurtenances of street parades, chariot races, herds of elephants, crowds of clowns, real tumbling, actual bareback riding, and all that. But not even Forepaugh's forty-horse team, or the dare devil performer riding alone and unarmed into the lion's cage, or the calliope can dim the luster and the magic of that first one-ring circus of Dan Rice in the vacant lot down by the grist mill.

This Detroit circus midway in 1898 featured, among other eye-catchers, "The Ferocious Untamable Lion," the "Original London Punch & Judy," and "The Wild Man" captured somewhere--probably in Wisconsin.

SANDWICHES & MAIN DISHES

CURRIED CHICKEN SALAD SANDWICHES

3 cups diced cooked chicken
1 cup diced celery
1 cup seedless green grapes, halved
1/2 cup sliced almonds
2 diced green onions
3 tablespoons lemon juice
1/2 cup mayonnaise
1/4 cup yogurt
2 teaspoons curry powder
Salt and pepper to taste
Pumpernickel bread

Mix chicken, celery, grapes, almonds and onions together. In a separate bowl, mix remaining ingredients. Pour dressing over chicken mixture and combine well. Chill before spreading on bread. (Makes 6 servings.)

EGG SALAD SANDWICHES

6 hard boiled eggs
1/4 cup chopped onion
1/4 cup chopped green pepper
1/3 cup mayonnaise
1 teaspoon salt
Dash or two of paprika

Mix eggs, onion and green pepper. Stir in mayonnaise and seasonings. (Makes 6 sandwiches.)

HAM SALAD SANDWICH SPREAD

1 slice onion
1 small sweet pickle, cut up
1/4 cup mayonnaise
1 teaspoon Worcestershire sauce
1 cup diced cooked ham

Process all ingredients, except ham, in a blender. Gradually add ham until just chopped.

BACON AND EGG SANDWICHES

(For all you campers who haven't discovered Holiday Inns yet.)

12 bacon strips, cooked and crumbled
5 chopped hard boiled eggs
1/4 cup chopped onion
1 cup shredded Swiss cheese
1/4 cup mayonnaise
2 tablespoons mustard
Salt and pepper to taste
Butter
12 slices bread

Mix bacon, eggs, onion, cheese, mayonnaise, mustard, salt and pepper. Refrigerate in a small container until ready to transfer into a cooler. Lightly butter one side of each bread slice. Spread bacon mixture on unbuttered side of 6 slices. Top with other 6 slices, butter on the outside. Fry until golden brown on both sides. (Makes 6 servings.)

58

GARDEN VEGETABLE POCKETS

(Go crazy and use any vegetable you want. This is just a start.)

4 cups shredded lettuce
1 diced stalk celery
1 large shredded carrot
1 chopped tomato, peeled and seeded
1/2 chopped green pepper
4-5 pocket breads
Ranch dressing

Combine vegetables in a bowl. Cut pocket breads in half and spoon in the vegetables. Pour dressing over the vegetables. (Makes 8 to 10.)

VEGETABLE CREAM CHEESE SANDWICHES

1 8-ounce package softened cream cheese
1/2 peeled cucumber, seeded and chopped
12 chopped red radishes
6 chopped green onions
Salt and pepper to taste
Dark, round pumpernickel bread

Mix together the cream cheese, cucumber, radishes and onions. Add the salt and pepper. Spread on pumpernickel bread. (Makes 4 sandwiches.)

FRIED PIKE WITH TOMATOES

(Great! Worth the hunt to find capers.)

4 pike fillets
1/3 cup flour
2 teaspoons tarragon
1 teaspoon salt
1/4 teaspoon pepper
1/3 cup butter
3 tomatoes, cut in wedges
1 teaspoon capers

Dip fillets in mixture of flour, tarragon, salt and pepper. Heat butter in a large skillet and fry fillets until golden. Turn and move to the side of skillet. Put tomatoes in skillet and sprinkle fish with the capers. Cook until tomatoes are hot and fish is flaky. (Makes 4 servings.)

BEER-BATTERED FISH

1 cup Bisquick
1 cup beer
Salt and pepper to taste
2-3 pounds of fillets
Oil for frying

Mix Bisquick, beer, salt and pepper in a pan. Dip fillets in mixture and fry in hot oil until golden brown. Drain on paper towels. (Makes 4-6 servings.)

DILL-GLAZED FISH

4 fish fillets
Oil for frying
1/2 cup butter, divided
2 cloves minced garlic
3 tablespoons lemon juice
3 tablespoons chopped fresh dill

Fry fillets in oil until tender and flaky. Remove to serving platter and keep hot. In another skillet saute 2 tablespoons of the butter and garlic for 1 minute. Lower heat and stir in lemon juice. Add in remaining butter and stir until melted. Remove from heat. Stir in dill. Pour over fillets. (Makes 4 servings.)

WHITEFISH AND ALMONDS

4 small-medium whitefish fillets
Salt and pepper
4 tablespoons butter
1 medium thinly-sliced onion
2 sliced lemons
Sliced almonds
Chopped fresh parsley

Season fillets with salt and pepper. Place on greased tin foil inside baking pan. Place pats of butter on each fillet. Cover with onion and lemon slices. Sprinkle with almonds and wrap foil tightly around fish. Bake at 350 degrees until fish is tender and flaky, about 35 minutes. Unwrap foil and sprinkle with parsley. (Makes 4 servings.)

CHICKEN-SPINACH STIR FRY

1/4 cup soy sauce
1 tablespoon sherry
1 tablespoon cornstarch
1 teaspoon sugar
2 cloves minced garlic
2 thin slices ginger root, minced
2 tablespoons oil
1 pound boneless chicken breasts, cut into strips
1 cup thinly sliced celery
1/2 pound spinach, stems removed,
and cut into bite-sized pieces
1 cup pea pods
1/4 cup sliced almonds

Combine soy sauce, sherry, cornstarch, sugar, garlic and ginger. Set aside. Heat oil in large skillet or wok. Stir in chicken. Saute for 2 minutes, or until just white. Add soy sauce mixture. Stir in celery, spinach and pea pods. Saute until vegetables are tender-crisp, about 2 minutes. Remove from heat. Stir in almonds. (Makes 4-6 servings.)

PASTA PRIMAVERA

(The nice thing about this dish is, like so many other vegetable recipes, you can use just about whatever vegetables you have on hand.)

2 tablespoons olive oil
3 cloves minced garlic
1 cup broccoli flowerettes
1 cup pea pods
2 shredded carrots
1/2 cup sliced mushrooms
1 small unpeeled zucchini, sliced
1 large diced tomato
4 tablespoons minced fresh parsley
1 tablespoon butter
1 tablespoon flour
1 1/2 cups milk
1/2 cup grated fresh Parmesan cheese
1/4 cup minced fresh basil
Salt and pepper to taste
12 ounces cooked linguini

Briefly saute garlic in oil. Add broccoli and pea pods, stirring until just tender (about 2-3 minutes). Stir in carrots, mushrooms and zucchini, sauteing another 2-3 minutes. Stir in tomato. Cover and remove from heat. In a saucepan, melt butter. Combine with flour to make a paste. Gradually stir in milk until sauce is slightly thickened. Stir in cheese and basil, heating until cheese melts. Add salt and pepper. In a large serving dish, gently mix linguini with vegetables and sauce. (Makes 4 servings.)

BARBECUED CHICKEN

2 cups cider vinegar
1 cup oil
1 tablespoon salt
2 teaspoons pepper
4 teaspoons poultry seasoning
2 chickens, split in half
2 well-beaten eggs

Mix vinegar, oil, salt, pepper and poultry seasoning together in a pan. Place chicken in mixture and marinate in refrigerator for 2-3 hours, occasionally spooning marinade over chicken. Put chicken on hot grill and cook slowly over medium hot coals. Mix eggs into marinade and brush over chicken. Turn chicken periodically and baste with marinade, making sure eggs are well-mixed. Grill until done, about 1 1/2-2 1/2 hours. (Makes 4-8 servings.)

PLUM BARBECUED RIBS

1 cup red wine
1/2 cup plum jam
1/4 cup oil
1/4 cup red wine vinegar
4 tablespoons soy sauce
3 cloves minced garlic
1 medium finely chopped onion
8 pounds spareribs

Combine all ingredients, except ribs, in a saucepan and heat until boiling, stirring constantly. Remove from heat. Place ribs in a pan and pour plum mixture on top. Refrigerate 3-4 hours or overnight, occasionally spooning marinade over ribs. Grill over medium hot coals, periodically basting with plum mixture. Grill until done, about 1-1 1/2 hours. (Makes about 8 servings.)

GRILLED PORK CHOPS

4 pork chops
4 halved tomatoes
8 large mushrooms
Oil
Salt and pepper to taste

Place chops on grill over medium hot coals. Grill, turning once, until chops are almost done, about 30 minutes. Place tomatoes and mushrooms on the grill between the chops. Brush vegetables with oil. Sprinkle with salt and pepper. Serve chops with vegetables on top. (Makes 4 servings.)

EASY ZUCCHINI QUICHE

3 cups grated zucchini
1 small chopped onion
1 cup Bisquick
4 well-beaten eggs
1/2 cup oil
3/4 cup grated Swiss cheese
1/2 teaspoon dried parsley
1/2 teaspoon dried marjoram
1/4 teaspoon salt
Fresh ground pepper to taste

Mix all ingredients together. Bake in a 10-inch greased pie pan at 350 degrees for 30-40 minutes, or until golden brown. (Makes 6 servings.)

Everyone kept his or her hat on while camping at Acme in the 1890s. Notice the man with the ax, watching the girl play the stringed instrument.

The Mystery
of
Gull Island

By *Harold Hawkins*

From the front porch of our cottage, the old house held a ghostly glow like a sentinel in an otherwise dark landscape. The point of land jutting out to our right and the peninsula extending beyond darkened the bay and the setting sun warmed only Gull Island some seven miles to the south. This island has intrigued me for a long time and I always knew that someday I would go there. I had seen it from many vantage points and the island held an air of mystery each time I viewed it.

Earlier in the day I had studied the island carefully from the overlook on the peninsula west of the small dot of land located on the nautical charts as being forty-five degrees, eight minutes latitude and eighty-five degrees, twenty-seven minutes longitude. Gull Island, itself, looked like a small gem mounted on a changing turquoise base. The house on the island faced toward the south and appeared to be immense. Two small buildings to the rear were hidden by vegetation except for the peaks which showed the ravages brought about by the droppings of the sea gulls. Stately trees adorned the windswept terrain. Looking at this scene through a strong pair of binoculars only served to whet my appetite to explore it.

I was thwarted in my first few attempts to reach Gull Island. The first time, a combination of choppy water and deep swells turned me back just two miles short of my goal. Each time I tried to approach the shore, Nature stepped in as if intent on keeping intruders away. The wind would suddenly shift, building heavy seas which would send me scurrying back into safe harbor at Northport. On one trip, about halfway out to the island, a fog bank rolled in completely hiding it from view. The fog was so dense I had to cut my engines and listen for the sounds of activity in the village in order to get my bearing.

Then one day Nature smiled and welcomed me to the island. A strong southwest wind had been blowing as a storm front wracked the mainland on the east side of the bay. The wind lessened and the bay became as smooth as polished marble. I was at the boatyard tinkering with the boat and as the bay flattened, giant black clouds made the most dramatic picture of the island I had ever seen. I felt an urgency to reach the scene before the magic was gone. I hurriedly cranked up the motor and headed out of the slip. Since there was no other traffic, I had smooth running as I sped toward my objective.

I thought of all the stories I had heard and realized that my curiosity would soon be satisfied. I thought of the house that had been built while the gulls were away during their mating season. Of how, when they returned, the builder brought cats to the island to keep the birds away, and of how the huge gulls picked up the cats and dropped them far out in the bay. And lastly, of how the family had been driven from the house they had built by thousands of screaming birds.

As I pulled around the western side of the island, the big house stood out starkly against the black sky. Tall fireplace chimneys graced the ends of the house and I could see the damage the droppings had caused. Part of the roof had rotted away showing the skeletal remains of the rafters. Most of the windows had been broken or had rotted from their frames. Lace curtains, grayed by age, floated slowly in and out as if propelled by some ghostly hand. Then I saw the gulls. Thousands upon thousands of them covered the beach and the sound of their cries was frightening. As I anchored the boat and waded ashore the birds rose like a giant cloud and darkened the sky. The flapping of their wings moved the still air and the stench was painful to my nostrils. I now understood the reason for the hasty retreat of the tenants who had tried to live there. The outbuildings were in the same state of disrepair as the house. I did not enter any of the buildings, fear of rotting floors forbade me, but everywhere I looked was devastation. Furnishings left were falling into decay and it was evident that the occupants had left hurriedly. Suddenly I felt the loneliness of that place of broken dreams. The house seemed to be a skull bared of its flesh, eyes vacant and forever staring. As I returned to the boat I took one last, lingering look. There was no mystery here. Man had encroached upon Nature, and Nature in anger had repelled him to keep the land inviolate for its own.

I felt a sadness as I rode back across the bay that evening, and yet I was strangely cheered by the thought that here, at least, everything had returned to the order for which it was intended.

"Sunday best" was the dress code in 1915 to go to Bob-Lo and ride the Merry-Go-Round.

VEGETABLES

EGGPLANT WITH CHEESE

1 medium quartered eggplant
4 beaten eggs
4 ounces farmer cheese
4 ounces cream cheese
4 tablespoons grated Parmesan cheese
1 teaspoon Italian seasoning
Butter

Boil eggplant until tender. Scoop out flesh, saving skins, and mix with remaining ingredients. Grease an 8-inch square pan. Line bottom of pan with eggplant skins. Spoon mixture over top and dot with butter. Bake at 350 degrees for about 40-45 minutes. (Makes 6 servings.)

GREEN BEANS AND TOMATOES

4 medium peeled tomatoes
1 pound cut up green beans
1 cup chopped onion
3 cloves minced garlic
2 tablespoons butter
1 tablespoon flour
1 teaspoon paprika

Cook tomatoes in salted water for 2 minutes. Add green beans and cook for 2 more minutes. Drain, saving 2 cups of liquid. Saute onion and garlic lightly in butter. Stir in flour and paprika. Slowly stir in 2 cups liquid, stirring constantly until sauce thickens slightly. Add vegetables, breaking up tomatoes. Cook over low heat for 5 minutes, stirring constantly. (Makes 4 servings.)

CHEESY POTATO SKINS

4 large baking potatoes
3 tablespoons melted butter
Garlic powder
1/4 cup grated cheddar cheese
Paprika

Bake potatoes at 425 degrees for 40-60 minutes. Cut potatoes into quarters and scoop out the potato, leaving a 1/4-inch shell. Place potatoes in a baking pan and brush with melted butter. Sprinkle with garlic powder, grated cheese and paprika. Bake 10-15 minutes, until crisp. If you like, you can sprinkle slightly cooked diced bacon on top before baking. (Makes 16 servings.)

POTATO AND PEA STIR FRY

1 1/2 pounds small unpeeled potatoes
1 teaspoon dried rosemary
3 tablespoons oil
1 1/2 cups fresh green peas, cooked 6 minutes
1 large red sweet pepper, cut into strips
3 tablespoons Dijon mustard
Salt and pepper to taste

Stir fry potatoes and rosemary in oil until potatoes are almost tender, about 8 minutes. Add peas and pepper, stirring mixture another 4 minutes. Stir in mustard, salt and pepper. (Makes 4 servings.)

ITALIAN ZUCCHINI

3 peeled and chopped tomatoes
1 cup corn
1/4 cup chopped onion
1/4 teaspoon Italian seasoning
Dash of onion and garlic powder
1 medium zucchini, sliced 1/4-inch thick

Bring tomatoes, corn, onion and seasonings to a boil. Lower heat and cook for 2 minutes. Add zucchini and cook another 3 minutes. (Makes 4 servings.)

CURRIED VEGETABLE STIR FRY

(You can use most any vegetable in this recipe. In addition, you can substitute soy sauce for the curry if you want a different flavor. Sometimes I sprinkle cheese over this and use it as a light, main dish.)

4 tablespoons olive oil
2 cups broccoli flowerettes
2 cups cauliflowerettes
1 cup sliced carrots
1 cup pea pods
1 cup shredded cabbage
1 medium cubed onion
1 cup sliced mushrooms
Curry powder to taste
(I use 1-2 tablespoons of the hot type)
1/4 cup sliced almonds

Stir fry the broccoli, cauliflower and carrots in the oil for about 2-3 minutes. Add the pea pods and cook another 2 minutes. Stir in cabbage, onion and mushrooms, cooking another 2-3 minutes. Stir in curry powder. Remove from heat and stir in sliced almonds. (Makes about 6-8 servings.)

CARROT AND CHEESE CASSEROLE

2 tablespoons softened butter
2 cups cooked and mashed carrots
2 beaten eggs
1/4 cup grated onion
Dash paprika
Salt and pepper to taste

Mix all ingredients together thoroughly. Spoon into an 8-inch square baking dish. Bake at 325 degrees for 40 minutes.

EGGPLANT PARMESAN

1 large peeled eggplant
Oil
3 medium peeled and chopped tomatoes
Salt
Oregano
3 cups shredded Monterey Jack cheese
1/4 cup grated Parmesan cheese

Cut eggplant into 1 1/4-inch slices. Fry until golden brown, about 5-7 minutes, in a skillet. Drain on paper towels. Layer 1/3 of the eggplant, tomatoes, dash of salt and oregano, and cheeses in a greased 9-inch square baking dish. Repeat, ending with cheese on top. Bake at 400 degrees for 40 minutes, or until top is lightly browned. Let stand 5-10 minutes before serving. (Makes 6-8 servings.)

LIMA BEAN AND CORN SUCCOTASH

2 cups shelled raw lima beans
2 cups cooked corn
4 tablespoons butter
Salt and pepper to taste

Cook beans until tender but not mushy, about 7 minutes. Drain. Mix in corn, butter, salt and pepper.

COOKOUT CORN

Pull back the husks and remove the silk from fresh ears of corn. Soak the cobs, husks and all, in cold water for 20-30 minutes. Drain the cobs. Dry and brush with melted butter. Tie the husks back in place. Roll each cob up in a piece of tin foil, sealing it tightly. Place in glowing coals and let it roast, turning several times, for 20-30 minutes, depending on size of the cob. Husk the corn. Add more melted butter along with salt and pepper. Get the next round ready.

SWEET AND SOUR GREEN BEANS

1 pound cut up green beans
2 tablespoons butter
2 tablespoons flour
2 tablespoons cider vinegar
1 tablespoon brown sugar

Cook green beans until tender, about 10 minutes, in 3 cups of salted water. Drain, keeping the cooking liquid. In a small saucepan melt the butter. Stir in the flour to make a paste. Stir in 2 cups of cooking water along with vinegar and sugar. Cook, stirring constantly, until mixture thickens. Pour the sauce on the beans and mix thoroughly. Simmer 5-6 minutes. (Makes 4-6 servings.)

TOMATO AND CORN CASSEROLE

1 1/4 cups crushed saltines
2 cups corn
1/4 cup minced onion
Salt and pepper to taste
4 tablespoons butter
3 sliced medium tomatoes
1 1/2 cups milk

Sprinkle 1/4 cup saltines in an 8-inch square baking dish. Dot with one tablespoon of the butter. In a small bowl, mix corn, onion, and salt and pepper. Spoon over crumbs. Place half the tomato slices on top. Sprinkle half the remaining crumbs on top. Dot with a tablespoon of butter. Repeat, ending with 2 tablespoons of the butter on the cracker crumbs. Bake at 400 degrees 30 minutes. (Makes 4 servings.)

CREAMY BAKED ONIONS

2 pounds peeled small onions
1/2 teaspoon salt
1/8 teaspoon pepper
1 1/4 cups half-and-half
3 tablespoons butter
1/2 cup grated cheddar cheese

Cook onions until tender. Drain and place in an 8-inch square baking dish. Sprinkle with salt and pepper. Pour half-and-half over onions. Dot with butter. Sprinkle with cheese. Bake covered at 350 degrees for 20 minutes. (Makes 6-8 servings.)

FRIED CABBAGE

Oil
3 cloves minced garlic
2 slices onion
1 pound cabbage, cut in 1/2-inch slices
Salt and pepper to taste

Saute garlic in oil. Stir in onion. Add cabbage, salt and pepper. Stir fry until cabbage is tender, about 10-12 minutes.

ZUCCHINI-CHEESE CASSEROLE

3 sliced medium zucchini
1/2 cup chopped onion
2 tablespoons oil
1 pound cottage cheese
1 teaspoon dried basil
1/2 teaspoon oregano
1/4 teaspoon salt
2 peeled and sliced tomatoes
1/3 cup grated Parmesan cheese

Saute zucchini and chopped onion in oil. Beat cottage cheese with basil, oregano and salt. Place alternating layers of zucchini, cottage cheese and tomatoes in a 2-quart casserole dish. Top with Parmesan cheese. Bake at 350 degrees uncovered for 25-30 minutes. (Makes 6 servings.)

PEAS IN SOUR CREAM

2 cups peas
1/4 cup water
1 teaspoon salt
1/2 teaspoon tarragon
Dash pepper
1/2 cup sour cream
1/2 cup mayonnaise
1 tablespoon lemon juice

Cook peas in water with salt, tarragon and pepper about 10 minutes. Heat sour cream, mayonnaise and lemon juice in double boiler, stirring frequently. Add drained peas and heat. (Makes 8 servings.)

Watermelon was a real treat in 1890, as these people at the Kebler Farm north of Grand Ledge proved.

Insect Life

By Caroline M. Kirkland

(The following is a chapter from <u>A New Home or Life In The Clearings</u> written in 1839. Kirkland's humorous book about life in Pinckney was so realistic in portraying the town and its people that she was forced to return with her family to New York City where she became editor of a magazine and continued with other writings.)

The day had been sultry, and, spite of the woods, our horses began to look fagged and weary before we reached the place where we intended to pass the night. The sun was in mighty power, as if he had forgotten it was four hours after noon, but certain attendant clouds had already begun to "lay their golden cushions down" in preparation for his *coucher.* The land now lay low and level, much intersected by small streams, and covered with the long grass of our rich savannahs. On these wide, grassy plains, great herds of cattle were feeding, or lying stretched in luxurious idleness under the scattered trees. We might have been surprised, such was the solitariness of the region, to find such numbers of these domestic animals; but we have not lived so long in the wilds without having discovered that a herd of cattle, with its tinkling bells, is not to be considered as a sign of close vicinity to the abodes of men. When cattle feed in wild and unfenced pastures, they soon exhaust or spoil those nearest home; and even without this excuse, they will often wander at their "own sweet will," till the chase after them at milking-time becomes no small part of the day's business.

"Hunting cattle *is* a dreadful chore!" remarked one of our neighbors, with piteous emphasis, after threading the country for three weeks in search of his best ox.

This is one of the characteristic troubles of new-country life. In vain is the far-sounding bell strapped round the neck of the master ox or cow, (for we say *master*-cow by catachresis I suppose.) A good bell may be heard by practiced ears four miles, if a valley or lake aid the transportation of sound; and a horse that has been accustomed to this species of coursing will prick up his ears and turn his head toward the sound of a well-known bell, thus serving as guide to the gudeman if he chance to be slow of hearing. Yet the herd will not always keep within bell sound. In vain too do we employ every ingenious artifice of temptation--supplying our "*salting-place*" with the great delicacy of the grazing people, and devoting the bran of each grist to the purpose of an extra feast, in the hope that the propensity to good feeding may overrule the national taste for unbounded liberty. "Home-bred memories" seem to have no place in the ruminations of the gregarious tribes. These expedients, which are resorted to only by the more provident, have indeed some efficacy, but they do not remedy the evil. It is sometimes mitigated by accidental causes.

When the flies become troublesome on the wide marshes, the whole herd, as if by previous agreement, will make for some well-known shade, near or distant, as the case may be, and there pass the sultry hours, only changing their positions gradually, as the sun throws the coveted shade eastward. And at the time of year when insects are most tormenting, the farmers make huge smokes in convenient spots near home, certain that to these all the cattle in the neighborhood will flock instinctively,--smoke being the best of all preventatives against flies and mosquitoes. So that, in the six weeks of mosquito-time, cattle-hunting becomes a less formidable "chore," and thus good comes out of evil. Evil! ay, the term is none too strong! I appeal to those who have traveled in the timbered land in July or August, I will not say to those who *live* in those regions, for I would fain hope their skin is hardened or armed in some way, as the fur of the ermine thickens and turns white in preparation for a Siberian winter.

One may observe, *en passant*, that ours is a rare region for the study of entomology. Those virtuosi who expend their amiable propensities in transfixing butter-flies and impaling gnats would here find ample employment from May until November. Indeed they might at times encounter more specimens than they could manage comfortably and without undue precipitation. First, in early April, appear, few and far between, the huge blue-bottle flies, slow-motioned and buzzy, as if they felt the dignity of their position as ancestors. Next in order, if I forget not, come the most minute of midges, silent and stealthy, pretending insignificance in order that they may sting the more securely. These seem to be ephemera, and fortunately the race soon runs out, at least they trouble us but for a short time.

Flies proper--honest, sincere flies--come on so gradually that we can hardly date their advent; but it is when sultry weather first begins, when the loaded clouds and the lambent lightning foretell the warm shower, that twitchings are seen,--and quick slaps are heard,--and these, with the addition of something very like muttered anathemas, announce the much-dreaded mosquito. Then come evenings--fortunately not long ones,--passed in the dark, lest the light should encourage the intruders. Moonlight is praised; and even this must be admired through closed sashes, unless we can contrive by the aid of closely-fitted gauze blinds to turn the house into a great safety-lamp,--we burning within its sultry precincts. Then are white walls spotted with human blood, like the den of some horrible ogre. Then "smudges" are in vogue,--heaps of damp combustibles placed on the windward side of the house and partially ignited, that their inky steams may smother the mosquitoes while we take our chance. I have had a "smudge" made in a chafing-dish at my bedside, after a serious deliberation between choking and being devoured at small mouthfuls, and I conscientiously recommend choking, or running the risk of it, at least.

If one wished to make a collection for a museum, nothing more would be necessary than to light a few candles on any hot night in August, especially when the weather is loud, and the open windows would be filled at once with a current of insect life, comprising all the varieties of *coleoptera* and their many-named kinsfolk; from the "shard-borne beetle with his drowsy wing," that goes knocking his back with unflinching pertinacity against every inch of the ceiling, to the "darning-needle," said to be an implement of Pluto himself, darting in all directions a body as long and, to all appearances, as useless as the sittings of our legislature.

We must not however claim preëminence for our dear Michigan in this particular point. The galli-nippers of Florida are said to have aided the Seminoles in appalling our armies, and we have of late heard of a prodigious number of bites in all parts of the Union. And do we not know from unquestionable historic authority, namely, that of a British tourist in America, that a presumptuous proboscis once dared to penetrate even General Washington's boots, as he rode through Newark marshes?

Our butterflies are nothing to boast of, and there are few of them with which one would be willing to change costumes, even to be "born in a bower." I have fancied that yellow predominates more than usual among them, and I have been tempted to believe they are bilious, like the rest of us. At any rate, the true ethereal and brilliant Psyche is but faintly represented by any specimen I have yet seen.

Mosquito-time, as before hinted, lasts, in its fury, but about six weeks, but flies are in season all summer. In the months of August and September particularly, black is the prevailing color of ceilings, looking-glasses and pictures, not to mention edibles of all classes. Much ingenuity is displayed in contriving what, in the paraphrastic tone of the day, we are bound to denominate destructive allurements for these intrusive and inconsiderate insects,--we used to call them fly-traps. These consist--in the more refined situations--of paper globes and draperies, delicately cut, so as to present externally an endless variety of cells and hiding-places, and these are well furnished within with poisoned sweets. Less fanciful people, frugal housewives and hard-hearted old bachelors,--place a large tumbler, partly filled with molasses, and covered with a piece of innocent-looking pasteboard having in the center a hole large enough for a blue-bottle to enter *toute déployée*, but affording a poor chance for escape after he has clogged his feet and wings in the too eager pur-suit of pleasure--a melancholy (and quite new) warning illustration of the *facilis descensus*. And again those of us who may by some chance have attended a course of chemistry, show our superior advantages by using a lit-tle water impregnated with cobalt, which carries swift destruction in every sip; and having at least the rec-ommendation of not being sticky, answers a very good purpose, unless the children happen to drink it.

Yet this ingenious variety of deaths makes no perceptible diminution in the number of our tormen-tors, and I have heard a good old lady exclaim against such contrivances altogether, saying that if you kill one fly, ten will be sure to come to his funeral.

Yet we must not be persuaded to fancy ourselves worse off than other people in this particular either. I remember well---and perhaps you too, reader--the ap-pearance of an elegant array of confectionery displayed in a verandah which hung over a lovely moonlit lake in a region where flies and midges had been for many years under the civilizing influences of good society. A blaze of light illumined the flower-wreathed pillars, and the gay crowd were ushered from the ballroom to the delicately furnished table, when lo! every article in sight appeared as if covered with black pepper; and the purest white and the most brilliant rainbow tints of creams and ices presented but one sad suit of iron gray. The very lights waxed dim in the saddened eyes of the gazers, for whole colonies of hapless gnats had found ruin in too warm a reception, and were reveng-ing themselves by extinguishing their destroyers.

But return we to our herds feeding beside the still waters.

Canoeing at Belle Isle near the Skating Pavilion around the turn of the century.

BREADS

PLUM MUFFINS

3/4 pound finely chopped plums
2 1/2 cups flour
2 teaspoons baking soda
1/2 teaspoon salt
1 cup sugar
1/4 cup melted butter
2 slightly beaten eggs
1/2 cup milk
1/2 cup chopped walnuts
1 tablespoon sugar

Sprinkle plums with 1 tablespoons flour and toss lightly. In a large bowl, combine flour, baking soda and salt with 1 cup sugar. In another bowl, mix the melted butter, eggs and milk, stirring until smooth. Add the liquid ingredients to the dry ones. Stir just until mixture is moistened. Fold in plums and walnuts. Spoon batter into greased muffin tins, filling about 2/3 full. Sprinkle the tablespoon of sugar on top of batter. Bake at 400 degrees for 20-25 minutes. (Makes 12-18 muffins.)

CHERRY BRAN MUFFINS

1 egg
1/2 cup milk
1/4 cup oil
1 cup pitted sour cherries
2 cups bran cereal
1/2 cup sugar
1/8 teaspoon salt
1 cup sifted flour
2 teaspoons baking powder
1/2 teaspoon nutmeg

Combine the egg, milk and oil. Stir in the cherries and cereal. Sift the sugar, salt, flour, baking powder and nutmeg. Add to the egg mixture. Fill greased muffin tins 2/3 full and bake at 400 degrees for about 20 minutes. (Makes about 12.)

BLUEBERRY MUFFINS

(One of my favorite standbys, these freeze well--if you can get people to keep their hands off long enough.)

2 1/2 cups flour
2 1/2 teaspoons baking powder
1/4 teaspoon salt
3/4 cup sugar, divided
1 cup buttermilk
2 beaten eggs
1/2 cup oil
1 1/2 cup blueberries

Sift together the flour, baking powder, salt and 1/2 cup sugar. In a separate bowl, combine the buttermilk, eggs and oil. Pour into the dry ingredients, mixing only until dry ingredients are dampened. Gently fold in berries (frozen ones work great). Spoon into greased muffins tins, filling 2/3 full. Sprinkle with remaining sugar. Bake at 400 degrees for 20-25 minutes. (Makes 12-16.)

PEAR BISCUITS

1 peeled pear, cored and cut up
1 teaspoon lemon juice
2 cups sifted flour
2 tablespoons sugar
1 tablespoon baking powder
1/2 teaspoon baking soda
1/4 teaspoon salt
4-6 tablespoons milk
6 tablespoons butter

Process the pear and lemon juice in a blender until smooth. In a medium bowl, mix together the flour, sugar, baking powder, baking soda and salt. Cut in butter until crumbly. Stir in the pear mixture. Add the milk, stirring until dough is slightly sticky. Pat dough out to a 1-inch thickness on a floured board. With a floured cutter or rim of a glass, cut into 2-inch rounds. Bake at 425 degrees until biscuits are light brown, about 15 minutes. (Makes about 12.)

STRAWBERRY BREAD

1/2 cup butter
1 cup sugar
1/2 teaspoon almond extract
2 eggs, separated
2 cups flour
1 teaspoon baking powder
1 teaspoon baking soda
1 teaspoon salt
1 cup crushed strawberries
1 tablespoon sugar

Cream butter, sugar and almond extract. Beat in egg yolks. Sift the flour, baking powder, soda and salt. Mix into creamed mixture alternately with strawberries. Beat egg whites until stiff. Fold into the batter. Pour into a greased loaf pan. Sprinkle sugar on top. Bake at 325 degrees for 50-60 minutes.

CARROT RAISIN BREAD

2 1/2 cups sifted flour
2 teaspoons baking powder
1 teaspoon baking soda
1 teaspoon cinnamon
1/4 teaspoon nutmeg
1/2 teaspoon salt
1 cup grated carrots
1 cup raisins
1/2 cup chopped walnuts
1 cup brown sugar
2 eggs
1 cup milk
1/2 cup melted butter

Mix together flour, baking powder, baking soda, cinnamon, nutmeg and salt. In a small bowl, stir carrots, raisins, walnuts and brown sugar. Beat eggs in large bowl; beat in milk and butter. Stir in carrot mixture. Add the flour mixture. Pour into a greased 6-cup Bundt pan. Bake at 350 degrees for about 1 hour. Cool on a rack for 5 minutes. Turn out onto a serving dish and let cool.

PEAR BREAD

1/2 cup butter
1 cup sugar
1 teaspoon vanilla
2 eggs
2 cups sifted flour
1/2 teaspoon salt
1/2 teaspoon baking soda
1 teaspoon baking powder
1/8 teaspoon nutmeg
1/4 cup sour cream
1 cup cored and coarsely chopped pears

Cream butter and sugar. Add the vanilla. Beat in eggs, one at a time. Combine dry ingredients. Stir into the creamed mixture. Mix in sour cream. Stir in the pears. Pour into a greased 9x5-inch loaf pan. Bake at 350 degrees for 1 hour.

PEACH COFFEECAKE

2 1/2 cups sifted flour
3/4 cup sugar
2 tablespoons baking powder
1/2 cup butter
2 eggs
2/3 cup milk
2 teaspoon vanilla
6 pitted and quartered peaches
Cream
1/3 cup sugar
1/2 cup flour
1 teaspoon cinnamon
3 tablespoons softened butter

Stir together the flour, sugar and baking powder. Cut in butter until crumbly. Beat together the eggs, milk and vanilla. Stir into the dry ingredients. Spoon into a greased 9-inch square baking pan. Place peach quarters on top and brush with some cream. In a small bowl, mix sugar, flour, cinnamon and butter until crumbly. Sprinkle over fruit. Bake at 375 degrees for 30 minutes.

CHEESE PANCAKES

1 pound farmer's cheese
2 tablespoons sour cream
2 eggs
3 tablespoons sugar
1/4 teaspoon salt
1/4 teaspoon vanilla
2-3 dashes cinnamon
1/2 cup flour
Butter
Powdered sugar
Sour cream
Jam or fruit syrup (optional)

Beat together the cheese, sour cream, eggs, sugar, salt, vanilla and cinnamon. Stir in the flour. Cover and chill well. Spoon about 2 tablespoons of batter into skillet containing sizzling butter, frying over medium heat until golden brown. Sprinkle with powdered sugar. Drop a spoonful of sour cream on top of each pancake. A spoonful of jam or fruit syrup may also be added, if desired. (Makes about 18-20 small pancakes.)

CHERRY PANCAKES

2 cups flour
1/2 cup sugar
1 tablespoon baking powder
1/2 teaspoon salt
2 eggs
1 cup milk
1/4 cup melted shortening
1 1/2 cup dried cherries
Butter

Sift the flour, sugar, baking powder and salt together. Beat the eggs, milk and shortening. Stir into the dry ingredients. Fold in the cherries. Spoon 2-3 tablespoons of batter into skillet containing sizzling butter. Fry over medium heat, turning when golden brown. (Makes 8-12 pancakes.)

This group of bathers is suitably dressed for swimming in the 1900s in South Haven. The Chicora is entering the harbor in the background.

The Bark-Covered House

By *John Nowlin*

(The following is a narrative of pioneer life in Dearborn in the 1830s.)

In raising our summer crops we had to do most of the work with a hoe. Sometimes where it was very rooty we planted corn with an ax. In order to do this we struck the blade into the ground and roots about two inches, then dropped the corn in and struck again two or three inches from the first place which closed it and the hull of corn was planted.

Now I must go back to the first season and tell how I got my first pig. It was the first of the hog species we owned in Michigan. Father went to the village and I with him. From there we went down to Mr. Thompson's (the man who moved us out from Detroit). He wished father to see his hogs. They went to the yard, and as was my habit, I followed along. Mr. Thompson called the hogs up. I thought he had some very fine ones. Among them was an old sow that had some beautiful pigs. She seemed to be very cross, raised her bristles and growled at us, as much as to say, "Let my pigs along."

I suppose Mr. Thompson thought he would have some sport with me, and being generous, he said: "If the boy will catch one I will give it to him." I selected one and started; I paid no attention to the old sow, but kept my eye on the pig I wanted, and the way I went for it was a caution. I caught it and ran for the fence, with the old sow after me. I got over very quickly and was safe with my pig in my arms. I started home, it kicked and squealed and tried to get away, but

I held it tightly, patted it and called it "piggy." I said to myself, "Now I have a pig of my own, it will soon grow up to be a hog, and we'll have pork." When I got home I put it in a barrel, covered it up so it could not get out and then took my ax, cut poles, and made it a new pen and put it on one place in Adam's world where pig and pig-pen had never been before. Now, thought I, I've got an ax, a pig and a gun.

One morning, a day or two after this, I went out and the pig was gone. Thinking it might have gone home, I went to Mr. Thompson's and inquired if they had seen it. I looked in the yard but the pig was not there. I made up my mind that it was lost, and started home. I followed the old trail, and when within sixty rods of the place where I now live, I met my pig. I was very glad to see it, but it turned from me and ran right into the woods. Now followed a chase which was very exciting to me. The pig seemed running for its life, I for my property, which was going off, over logs and through the brush, as fast as its legs could carry it. It was a hard chase, but I caught the pig and took it back. I made the pen stronger, and put it in again, but it would not eat much and in a few days after died, and away went all my imaginary pork.

Mr. Pardee had bought a piece of land for a Mr. Clapp, of Peekskill, New York, and was agent for the same. He said the south end of this land was openings. It was about one mile from our place, and Mr. Pardee offered to join with father and put corn on it, accordingly, we went to see it. There was some brush, but it was mostly covered with what we called "buffalo grass," which grew spontaneously. Cattle loved it very much in the summer, but their grazing it seemed to destroy it. It soon died out and mostly disappeared, scrub-oak and other brush coming up in its place.

Mr. Pardee and father soon cleared five or six acres of this land, and with the brush they cut made a light brush fence around it, then tore up three or four acres and planted it with corn. The soil was light yellow sand. When the corn came up it was small and yellow. They put in about two acres of buckwheat. A young man by the name of William Beal worked for Pardee. He helped to tend the corn. One morning, as they were going up to hoe the corn, William Beal took his gun and started ahead; this he frequently did very early. He said, when about half way to the corn, he looked toward the creek and saw a black bear coming toward him. He stood in the path, leading to the cornfield, which they had underbrushed. The bear did not discover him until he was near enough, when he fired and shot him dead. This raised quite an excitement among us. I went to see the bear. It was the first wild one I saw in Michigan. They dressed it, and so far as I know, the neighbors each had a piece; at all events, we had some.

They hoed the corn once or twice, and then made up their minds it was no use, as it would not amount to much, the land being too poor. The whole crop of corn, gathered there, green at that, nubbins and all, was put into a half bushel handle basket, excepting what the squirrels took.

The buckwheat didn't amount to much, either. Wild turkeys trampled it down and ate the grain, in doing which, many of them lost their lives. I began to consider myself quite a marksman. I had already, with father's rifle, shot two deer, and had gotten some of the turkeys.

Father never cropped it any more on the openings, and his experience there made him much more pleased with his own farm. That land is near me, and I have seen a great many crops growing on it, both grain and other crops, but never one which I thought would pay the husbandman for his labor.

Father's partnership with Mr. Pardee was so unsuccessful on the openings, and in having to take the oxen back, and buy hay for them when that article was very high (their running out helped him some) that he concluded to go into partnership with Mr. Pardee, no more.

He sold half of his oxen to Asa Blare, who paid the money down, so their partnership opened in a little better shape. This partnership, father said, was necessary as our money had become very much reduced, and everything we bought, (such as flour and pork) was extremely dear; besides, we had no way to make a farthing except with our "maple-sweet" or the hide of a deer.

Father could not get work, for there were but few settlers, and none near him, who were able to hire. So he economized to save his money as much as possible, and worked at home. The clearing near the house grew larger and larger, and now we could see the beautiful sun earlier.

Father worked very hard, got three acres cleared and ready for wheat. Then he went away and bought about four bushels of white wheat for seed. This cost a snug sum in those days. About the last of August he sowed it and dragged it in with his drag. He sowed about a bushel and a peck to the acre. (I have for many years back, and to the present time, sowed two bushels to the acre.)

His wheat came up and looked beautiful. The next spring and early summer it was very nice. One day a neighbor's unruly ox broke into it. I went through it to drive him out and it was knee high. Father said take the ox home. I did so. The neighbor was eating dinner. I told him his ox had been in our wheat and that father wished him to keep the ox away. He said we must make the fence better and he would not get in. This was the first unkind word I had received from a neighbor in Michigan. The wheat escaped the rust, headed and filled well and was excellent crop. It helped us a great deal and was our manna in the wilderness.

Father and I continued our chopping until we connected the two clearings. Then we commenced to see the sun in the morning and we thought it shone brighter here than it did in York State. Some of the neighbors said that it really did, and that it might be on account of a reflection from the water of the great lakes. Perhaps it was because the deep gloom of the forest had shaded us so long and was now removed. Israel like, we looked back and longed for the good things we had left, viz;--apples, pears and the quince sauce. Even apples were luxuries we could not have and we greatly missed them. We cleared new ground, sowed turnip seed, dragged it in and raised some very large nice turnips. At this time there was not a wagon in the neighborhood, but Mr. Travis, being a mechanic and ingenious, cut down a tree, sawed off two short logs, used them for hubs and made the wheels for a cart. These he took to Dearbornville and had them ironed off. He made the body himself and then had an ox-cart. This was the only wheeled vehicle in the place for some years. As Mr. Travis was an obliging man the neighbors borrowed his cart. Sometimes it went to Dearbornville to bring in provision, or other things, and sometimes it went to mill. (There was a mill on the River Rouge, one mile north of Dearbornville.) With this cart and oxen the neighbors carried some of their first products, sugar, butter, eggs, &c, to Detroit. Some young sightseers, who had not seen Detroit since they moved into the woods and wished to see it, were on board. They had to start before midnight so it would be cool traveling for the oxen. This was the first cart and oxen ever seen in Detroit from our part of the town of Dearborn.

They reached home the following night, at about ten o'clock, and told me about the trip.

We wanted apples, so father took his oxen, went and borrowed the cart, loaded it with turnips, went down the river road half way to Detroit, traded them with a Frenchman for apples and brought home a load which were to us delicious fruit. In this way we got our apples for many years. These apples were small, not so large and nice as those we had been used to having; but they were Michigan apples and we appreciated them very much. They lasted us through the winter and did us much good.

Smile, flappers. This group in the daring bathing suits posed outside the casino at South Haven in the mid-1920s.

DESSERTS

MACKINAC ISLAND FUDGE

(For chocolate fudge, add 1 1-ounce square of bitter chocolate to the boiling mixture.)

1/2 cup milk
1/2 cup butter
1/2 cup brown sugar
1/2 cup white sugar
Dash salt
1 teaspoon vanilla
2 cups powdered sugar

Mix milk, butter, sugars and salt in a heavy saucepan. Cook over medium heat and bring to a boil, stirring constantly. Boil 6 minutes, stirring all the while. Remove from heat. Add vanilla and powdered sugar. Beat with a mixer until smooth and thick, about 6 minutes. Pour into a buttered pan and freeze for 20 minutes. Cut into pieces. (Makes a little more than a pound.)

STRAWBERRY PUDDING

3 cups hulled strawberries
1 cup sugar
1/2 cup water
6 slices firm white bread
Butter
Sweetened whipped cream

Cook strawberries, sugar and water. Butter bread on one side. Cut into quarters. Alternate layers of bread and strawberry mixture in a loaf pan. Chill. Slice and serve with whipped cream.

PEACHES AND YOGURT

6 sliced medium peaches
4 tablespoons wheat germ
1/2 teaspoon ground ginger
2 cups plain yogurt
1/2 cup brown sugar

Mix together peaches, wheat germ and ginger. In another bowl combine yogurt and sugar. Stir into peach mixture. (Makes 6-8 servings.)

PEACHES AND CREAM

6 pitted and quartered peaches
1 1/2 cups water
1 1/2 cups sugar
8 cloves
2-inch stick cinnamon
1/4 cup orange-flavored liqueur
Sweetened whipped cream

Boil the water, sugar and spices together for 3 minutes. Add the peaches and simmer until fruit is tender, about 6 minutes. Remove from heat. Stir in liqueur. Pour mixture into a bowl and chill. To serve, spoon fruit into individual serving bowls. Top with whipped cream. (Makes 6 servings.)

SHERRIED CUSTARD AND FRUIT

1/4 cup sugar
2 tablespoons cornstarch
Dash of salt
1 cup half-and-half
1 cup milk
1/4 cup sherry
2 beaten egg yolks
2 tablespoons butter
1 teaspoon vanilla
2 cups fresh fruit
(strawberries, raspberries, blueberries or peaches)

Mix sugar, cornstarch and salt together in a saucepan. Stir in half-and-half, milk and sherry, blending well. Cook over medium heat, stirring constantly, until mixture boils. Boil for 1 minute. Remove from heat. Stir a small portion of the sauce into egg yolks. Pour yolks into pan and cook for 1 minute, stirring constantly. Remove from heat and add butter and vanilla. Cool. Spoon custard over fruit in dessert dishes. (Makes 4 servings.)

GRAPE CREAM

2 cups seedless green grapes
1/2 cup sour cream
2 tablespoons brown sugar
1/4 teaspoon ginger

Place grapes in a serving bowl. Dab on cream. Mix brown sugar and ginger together. Sprinkle over cream. (Makes 4 servings.)

MELON PIE

9-inch baked pie shell
1 3-ounce package lemon gelatin
1 cup well-drained, cubed cantaloupe
1 cup well-drained, cubed watermelon
1 cup well-drained, cubed honeydew melon
1/2 cup heavy cream, whipped

Prepare gelatin according to package directions, using only 1 1/2 cups of water. Chill until slightly thickened. Fold whipped cream and melons into gelatin. Pour into baked pastry shell. Chill several hours or until firm.

RASPBERRY-CHERRY ICE

2 pints pureed raspberries
(strain to remove seeds)
1 cup sugar
4 tablespoons cherry brandy

Mix raspberries, sugar and brandy together until sugar dissolves. Freeze in a shallow pan until almost set, about 1 hour. Stir until thoroughly mixed. Return to freezer and chill until almost firm, about 1-1 1/2 hours. Serve in individual dessert dishes.

STRAWBERRY GRAHAM CAKE

3/2 cup sugar, divided
1/4 cup oil
3 cups sliced strawberries, divided
1 cup sliced almonds
Pinch of cinnamon
3 egg whites
36 graham cracker squares
1 cup sweetened whipped cream
Graham cracker crumbs
Crushed almonds

In a large bowl, mix together 1/2 cup sugar, oil, strawberries and sliced almonds. In a small bowl, beat egg whites until soft peaks form. Gradually add remaining sugar until stiff peaks form. Gently fold in strawberry mixture. Lay 9 graham crackers on the bottom of an 8-inch square baking dish. Spread one-third of the strawberry mixture over this. Top with another layer of crackers. Repeat 2 more times, ending with crackers on top. Cover and chill thoroughly. Before serving, spread with whipped cream and sprinkle with a mixture of graham cracker crumbs and crushed almonds. (Makes 9 servings.)

RASPBERRY-ALMOND ICE CREAM

(Dust off those ice cream makers!)

1/2 cup half-and-half
2/3 cup sugar
2 teaspoons unflavored softened gelatin
Pinch of salt
2 cups whipped cream
1 cup pureed raspberries
(strain to remove seeds)
1/2 teaspoon almond extract

Heat half-and-half in a double boiler. Add sugar, gelatin and salt, stirring constantly until dissolved. Remove from heat and stir in cream. Cool. Stir in berries and almond extract. Chill 1-2 hours. Churn in ice cream maker.

STRAWBERRY SHORTBREADS

1/2 cup butter
1/4 cup sugar
1 1/4 cups flour
1 1/2 cup raspberries
1 cup sweetened whipped cream

Cream butter. Gradually add the sugar. Stir in the flour. Chill thoroughly. Roll out dough on floured board to 1/8-inch thickness. Cut out 6 3-inch rounds and 6 2-inch rounds. Place on a baking sheet and bake at 350 degrees for 15-20 minutes, or until barely brown. Reserve 6 raspberries. Fold remaining berries into whipped cream. To serve, place a large shortbread on each dessert dish. Put a spoonful of raspberry whipped cream over cookie. Top with smaller short-bread. Put a dab of cream on top and garnish with a whole berry. (Makes 6 servings.)

PEACH BROWN BETTY

8 peeled medium peaches, pitted and sliced
3 tablespoons lemon juice
4 slices of white bread
4 tablespoons butter
1/2 cup brown sugar
1/2 teaspoon cinnamon
Dash of nutmeg
1/2 teaspoon grated lemon rind
1/2 cup water

Mix the peach slices with lemon juice. Butter the bread and cut into small cubes, measuring enough to makes 1 1/4 cups. Grease a 1 1/2-quart baking dish and sprinkle about 1/4 cup of the bread cubes in the bottom. Top with half the peach slices. Mix sugar, cinnamon, nutmeg and lemon rind together. Sprinkle half this mixture over peach slices. Layer in remaining peaches and top with sugar mixture. Pour in the water. Place remaining bread cubes on top. Cover and bake at 400 degrees for 15 minutes. Uncover and bake about 30 minutes longer, or until golden brown. (Makes 6 servings.)

BLUEBERRY-CREAM CAKE

3 cups sifted flour
1/4 teaspoon salt
Dash of cinnamon
1 tablespoon baking powder
2/3 cup butter
1 cup sugar, divided
1 teaspoon vanilla
1 cup water
4 egg whites
1 8-ounce package cream cheese
3 tablespoons milk
3 tablespoons sugar
1/2 cup currant jelly
2 cups blueberries
1 cup heavy cream
(whipped and sweetened to taste)

Combine flour, salt, cinnamon and baking powder. Cream butter and sugar until light and fluffy. Beat in vanilla. Add alternately with water to flour mixture, beating until well-blended. Beat egg whites until stiff and fold into batter. Spoon into greased 13x9-inch baking dish. Bake at 350 degrees for 30 minutes. Beat cream cheese with milk and sugar. Spread over cooled cake. Melt jelly in a saucepan. Remove from heat and stir in blueberries. Cool slightly and spoon over cream cheese. Cover cake with sweetened whipped cream.

BLUEBERRY DUMPLING DESSERT

1 cup sifted flour
3 tablespoons sugar
2 teaspoons baking powder
1/4 teaspoon salt
Dash of cinnamon
1 tablespoon butter
2 1/2 cups blueberries
1/3 cup sugar
1 tablespoon lemon juice
1/2 cup milk
Sweetened whipped cream

Mix together the flour, 3 tablespoons sugar, baking powder, salt and cinnamon. Cut in the butter to make coarse crumbs. Add milk, stirring until moistened. Set aside. Boil together in a large saucepan the blueberries, 1/3 cup sugar and lemon juice. Lower heat to simmer. Cover and cook 5 minutes. Drop 6 spoonfuls of dough mixture onto the simmering blueberries. Cover tightly and cook over low heat for 10 minutes. Serve with sweetened whipped cream.

The mode of transportation on Mackinac Island hasn't changed much since this photo was shot.

Reminiscences
of Early Days
on Mackinac Island

By Elizabeth Therese Baird

*(The following are two narratives about life on Macki-
nac Island in the 1820s. The first describes Mrs. David
Mitchell, an Ottawa woman who married a British army
surgeon, and the crops grown on the Island. The second describes the wedding of Edward Biddle and a Native American, step-daughter of Joseph Bailly, a French
fur trader.)*

Mrs. David Mitchell

Mrs. David Mitchell owned and cultivated a large
farm on the southwest side of the island. It might be
called a hay farm, as hay was the principal and always a
large crop. Hay was a very expensive article at Mackinac, at that time. It was customary for men to go to the
surrounding islands, mow what grass they could
among the bushes, remain there until the hay was
cured, then return for boats to convey it to Mackinac.
Potatoes were also largely cultivated by Mrs. Mitchell,
and "Mackinac potatoes" were regarded as the choicest
in this part of the country. Oats and corn were also
raised. An attempt was made to raise fruit trees, but
with small success; these did better in town. The farm
house was comfortable-looking, one story in height,
painted white, with green blinds; a long porch ran
across the front. This house stood in about the center
of the farm, far back from the road. The farm was not-
ed also for its fine springs. Then there was Mrs.
Mitchell's garden, which lay between the bluff, or hill,
and the lake; on one side lay the government garden,
and on the other was "the point." It was a large plot,

two or three acres in extent, and was entirely enclosed by cedar pickets five feet high, whitewashed, as were all enclosures at Mackinac. All vegetables that would grow in so cold a climate were cultivated. It was an every-day occurrence to see Mrs. Mitchell coming to inspect her garden, riding in her calash, a two-wheeled vehicle, being her own driver. When the old lady arrived the men would hasten to open the gate, then she would drive in; and there, in the large space in front of the garden beds, in the shade, the man would fasten the horse, while "my lady" would walk all over the grounds giving her orders. The refuse of this garden, the rakings, etc., were carried to the shore and made a conspicuous dark spot, like an island on the white beach, which in later years grew into a considerable point and was covered with verdure.

Her speech was peculiar. English she could not speak at all, but would mix the French with her own language, which was neither Ottawa nor Chippewa. There were not many who could understand her; there was, however, one old man who had lived for a great many years with the family, who was a natural interpreter and seemed perfectly to comprehend her. And yet, she got along admirably in company. She had many signs that were expressive, and managed to make her wishes clear to the ladies. When her daughters were at home, her linguistic troubles vanished. She was quite large, tall, and heavy. Her dress was as peculiar as her conversation. She always wore black,--usually her dresses were of black silk, which were always made in the same manner. A full skirt was gathered and attached to a plain waist. There were two large pockets on the skirt, and she always stood with her hands in these. About her neck was a black neckerchief; on her head she wore a black beaver hat, with a modest plume at one side. There were ties, but nowhere else on the bonnet was ribbon used. This bonnet she wore day and night. I do not think she slept in it, but never did I know of any one who had ever seen her without it. She was an intelligent woman, with exceptional business faculties, although devoid of book-learning. Her skill in reading character was considerable. Such was the "Mistress of the manse."

The Wedding

In the course of time there came to the island of Mackinac, a young man from the East, who was of an old and honored family of Philadelphia. He was a brother of Nicholas Biddle, president of the United States Bank during the administration of Andrew Jackson, and a relative of Commodore Biddle.

Edward Biddle became very much attached to an Indian girl. The attachment warmed into a sincere love on both sides. He did not know her language, neither did she understand his; but love needed no tongue. In 1819 they were married at her step-father's home. The ceremony was performed by the notary public, Samuel Abbott, who for years was the only functionary there invested with the necessary authority for that purpose.

Would that my pen might do justice to this wedding! It was most picturesque, yet no one can fully understand its attractiveness and novelty without some description of the style of dress worn by the bride and others of the women: a double skirt made of fine narrow broadcloth, with but one pleat on each side; no fullness in front nor in the back. The skirt reached about half-way between the ankle and the knee, and was elaborately embroidered with ribbon and beads on both the lower and upper edges. On the lower, the width of the trimming was six inches, and on the upper, five inches. The same trimming extended up the overlapping edge of the skirt. Above this horizontal trimming were rows upon rows of ribbon, four or five inches wide, placed so near together that only a narrow strip of the cloth showed, like a narrow cord. Accompanying this was worn a pair of leggins made of broadcloth. When the skirt is black, the leggins are of scarlet broadcloth, the embroidery about three inches from the side edge. Around the bottom the trimming is between four and five inches in width. The moccasins, also, were embroidered with ribbon and beads. Then we come to the blanket, as it is called, which is of fine broadcloth, either black or red, with most elaborate work of ribbon; no beads, however, are used on it. This is worn somewhat as the Spanish women wear their mantles. The waist, or sacque, is a sort of loose-fitting garment made of silk for extra occasions, but usually of calico. It is made plain, without either embroidery of ribbon or beads. The sleeves snugly fit the arm and wrist, and the neck has only a binding to finish it. Beads enough are worn around the neck to fill in and come down in front. Silver brooches are worn according to taste. The hair is worn plain, parted in the middle, braided down the back, and tied up again, making a double *queue*. At this wedding, four such dresses appeared-- those of the bride, her mother, Madame Laframboise, and Madame Schindler.

Urban sprawl at Interlochen State Park in 1932. Is everyone having a great time? You bet.

INDEX

VEGETABLES

BREADS

DESSERTS

Michigan Summers

This bathing scene was shot from the North Pier at South Haven in 1910. Did anyone actually swim, or did they just stand around a lot?

Other Eberly Press Books

Christmas in Michigan: Tales & Recipes

The 12th floor of Hudson's. The smell of a freshly-cut pine tree. Chocolate Santas from Sanders. This is Christmas in Michigan. Stories about Christmas in our Great Lakes State. Historical recipes from turn-of-the-century church and community cookbooks. $6.95

Michigan Cooking...and Other Things

A unique collection of Michigan recipes, witty articles by Michigan writers and illustrations of Michigan points of interest. $4.95

More Michigan Cooking...and Other Things

The best yet to come. All new recipes, illustrations and humor about life in Michigan. $4.95

Our Michigan: Ethnic Tales & Recipes

Recipes for Canadian butter tarts, Czech kolache, Hungarian Linzer slices, Irish coffee, Polish pierogie and 150 more ethnic dishes. Tales about and by the people who settled Michigan from all over the world. Historical photos. $6.95

Brownie Recipes

Cream cheese brownie supreme, double frosted bourbon brownies, Jessica's mocha-mint caramel downfall...and more than 170 others. Throw out your bathroom scale, destroy those calorie-counting books, move your waistband over another inch. $5.95

101 Apple Recipes

Apple pizza, apple quiche, paper bag apple pie, you name it--it's here. $2.50

101 Vegetable Recipes

The book that tells you how to turn that ten-pound zucchini into something edible. The book you can count on when it's your turn to bring the vegetable dish to the school picnic. $2.50

101 Fruit Recipes

Such fruity delights as German apple pancake, apricot coconut chews, blueberry coffeecake, pear pie and peach pecan pie. $2.50

101 Cherry Recipes

Cherry bounce, black cherry biscuits, cherry brandy, cherry cheese pie...dozens more. $2.50

101 Strawberry Recipes

Lazy day strawberry cream pie, strawberry biscuits, strawberry mousse, strawberry thumbprint cookies, Fourth of July pie, strawberry torte...lots more. $2.50

Wild Mushroom Recipes

A charming little book filled with recipes for your mushrooming friends--and yourself. Mushroom caviar, mushroom quiche, cream of mushroom soup. $2.00

Michigan Puzzles

Crossword puzzles, secret codes, etc. all based on Michigan's well and little-known facts. Fun for children 10 to 110. $1.75

Early American Recipes

Irish coffee pudding, Shaker lemon pie, hot mustard bread, switchel, Southern spiced tea, dozens more mouth-watering recipes compiled into complete menus by a Greenfield Village cooking instructor. $4.95

How to Heat & Eat With Woodburning Stoves

A book covering such items as choosing a stove, installation, safety tips, add-on gizmos and more than 150 easy-to-use recipes. $4.95

eberly press
1004 Michigan Ave.
E. Lansing, MI 48823

Please include $2 for each order of two books or less for postage and handling. When ordering three books or more, please add $3.

Carole Eberly, with daughter Jessica, on vacation in a log cabin overlooking Crystal Lake near Frankfort in 1980.

About the Author

Carole Eberly is a former legislative reporter for United Press International. A freelance writer and editor, she is also a faculty member at Michigan State University's School of Journalism. Besides cooking and eating, Carole's hobbies include running, watching movies (with a large tub of popcorn), playing with her two cats, finding great bargains at garage sales, and traveling around Michigan.

Notes

Notes

Notes

Notes